LIFESTORY

THIS IS **THE** LIFESTORY OF

_____

FROM

_____

BEGUN ON

_____

LIFESTORY

First published in the Republic of Ireland in 2006 by
The Irish Hospice Foundation
Morrison Chambers, 32 Nassau Street, Dublin 2, Ireland

Designed by Ed Miliano
Edited by John Waters

Printed by Everbest Printing Co. Ltd
on 150 gsm Munken Pure and typeset in Trinité No. 3

ISBN 0-9534880-4-7

THE IRISH
HOSPICE
FOUNDATION

LIFESTORY

CONTENTS

LET YOUR STAR SHINE

BY MAEVE BINCHY

YOU ARE A HERO.

AND I AM A HERO.

WHY?

BECAUSE WE HAVE IN OUR

HANDS A BOOK IN WHICH

WE ARE GOING TO STAR.

Could anything be more marvellous? Nobody is going to ask us to tone it down, to be less self-centred, to make more room for others. This is the one chance where we are positively *encouraged* to be centre stage. Miss it at your peril. Never again will they beg you to come out and take your place in the limelight. Oh, how I wish they had a book like this when my parents were young. I have no idea what their first day of work was like in those far gone times, one as a nurse in a Dublin hospital and the other in the Law Library at the Four Courts. Or who their friends were at school and how they spent their First Communion Days. I wish I knew what they hoped for and talked about as they set out from Dún Laoghaire on their honeymoon aboard the mail boat with a crowd of people in horrific 1930s clothes waving from the pier.

And suppose books like this had been the common currency of historical figures, look at how much we would have known about the mindset of so many people we can only guess about. Did Alexander *know* he was 'the Great'? Did St Francis always like animals even when he was a child? Was Judy Garland *ever* happy? Did Wolfe Tone think his dream would come true in one generation? If they had filled in a book like this, we would be able to make a much more educated guess. But these books are not intended *only* for the famous. They are for everyone. We are the centre of the story.

As a storyteller I spend a great deal of time watching people. I used to follow them about long ago. But since I am no longer very mobile I watch nowadays from a seat in a shopping mall, a table in a café, a booth in a bar, a bench in an airport, or a parked car on a suburban street. I have never been bored, not once, as I sit and watch the people who are the heroes of their own life stories walk by.

There's the woman of fifty patting her hair and looking at her reflection in the windows she passes. She had a spring in her step yet her eyes were wary. Maybe she was going on her first Lonely Hearts date and is hoping she has not over-sold herself. Or possibly she has been invited out to lunch by her first boyfriend whom she hasn't seen for thirty years. Or maybe the dull unemotional husband had told her that he needed her and she's wondering will it last. Perhaps it has nothing to do with love and she has just got her pilot's licence, made her first million, or had a poem published. Or none of these things.

But it does prove that when you watch people and wonder about them their lives can never be dull. And how much more interesting still when the story is about ourselves!

I can't wait to get started on this book and I have vowed that I will be honest. It will not be a succession of triumphant times like those letters people write with a Christmas card telling you how brilliantly well each and every member of the family is doing. It will not be a catalogue of perfectly wonderful characters all described in glowing terms in case they read it when I am dead. I won't pretend to have been happy *all* of the time because no one is or was and it would be sickening for anyone else to read and unreal for me to read myself. So I will write about my first day at school when we were asked to fill a page with drawings of pot hooks, and I did one giant pot hook which filled the page and went to get my coat and satchel to go home with the air of a day's work done well and speedily. And how the others had sniggered into their hands.

And much later my Confirmation Day where I was a foot taller than all the other pupils and because we wore ordinary clothes and weren't dressed up like a May altar, I was mistakenly ushered into a pew with the teachers and parents and had to fight my way out to be confirmed.

And there was the day I got the Leaving Certificate and to celebrate this huge achievement my parents took the whole family to Jammet's which was the poshest restaurant in Dublin and totally out of our league. My mother, normally so relaxed and confident, hissed to the four of us children that if any of us began to eat the bread rolls on the table she would saw our hands

off at the wrist. My father didn't have quite enough money for the bill. And so we all sat glumly wishing for the nice happy meal we would have had at home instead of this.

When I was eighteen I stayed in a hotel for the first time. It was a place in London's Cromwell Road. I didn't know whether you should make the bed or not. It was a huge puzzlement. If you didn't then they might think you were a tramp, if you did they might think you were too humble and servile. I worked it out that by sort of folding it back neatly I couldn't be accused of either. I was too afraid to ask anyone for years in case they thought I was an eejit and always folded back. I still do.

I think I'll write about our hens. Elderly hens called Celeste and Adrienne and Gillian and Sylvia – after my friends at school. One day one of them fell dead from the perch and my marvellous mother, who could have run the world, took the dead hen in to the Department of Agriculture in case it might have had fowl pest and we could get compensation. When she told the man that the hen in the cornflake box was fifteen and a half years old, he got a fit of laughing and whooping and spluttering and had to be helped from his office. My mother took this as a 'no' as regards compensation and she brought the hen home on the bus to be buried with hymns in the raspberry bushes.

And I could write about how I once thought I would be a saint and there would be a Saint Maeve's Day but I didn't want to be a martyr and said a prayer every day asking to be excused martyrdom. And so far I have been. Then I hoped to be the first woman judge in Ireland but fortunately realised after two months that Law was not for me. I absolutely loved teaching and I spent eight happy years in classrooms and I was even going to run my own school in my mind.

And I travelled the world in the vacations, coming back with a sun tan, mosquito bites and a great sense of restlessness about two hours before term started in September.

And I fell in love with fellows who often wrongly and strangely didn't fancy me at all and a few who unwisely did, and my mother said that if I was a bit quieter, dressed up and went to Irish seaside resorts instead of minding children in a camp in New York State, sleeping on the deck of a ship to the Far East and plucking chickens in a kibbutz I might meet someone suitable.

But I never got quiet or went to Rosslare and then in my early thirties I met Gordon, a great man who was very suitable and *did* love me back, and just as all our life stories are fascinating to us, we must remember that the story of who we love would actually bore the teeth out of anyone else but is very special to us so that will all go in the book as well.

I have never written a real autobiography or memoir. For many reasons. Our childhood belongs to the four of us. I don't want to hijack it and say – this is the way it was. Also it was a very happy life and these are great to live but fairly tedious to read about. When I hear of idyllic family picnics, long summer evenings in a big garden with the hens clucking and the rabbits in a hutch woffling their little noses, and winter evenings by the fire where the big treat was to be allowed to stay up for *Saturday Night*

Theatre on BBC radio . . . well it makes me want to ask for the sick bag. Such complacency and smugness.

Come on.

We much prefer to read about misery in the home, poverty, alcoholism, strain. But we just didn't *have* that, we had security and just enough money to educate us all so we were lucky, very lucky, and it's hard to write about that without sounding like a crowing cock.

I can see a series of big jolly Christmas Days where my parents would invite anyone who might not have a nice place to go for Christmas.

All those summers where they would rent a house for us all in Ballybunion for a month. The house cost thirty pounds a month, which was astronomical in those days, and we all had to get value from the holiday by throwing ourselves into the Atlantic. Imagine, Daddy had spent a pound a day for the seven of us to have a holiday: of course we had to get into the freezing sea.

So this will be it – this book will be my autobiography, which the family can look at as the years go by, and maybe they'll write theirs too.

I am certainly going to give this book as a present to people and encourage them to sit down and remember. To hunt for the photographs that tell a story. I think that a book like this will make sense of our lives. It will chart the journey we are taking, rescue memories from a jumble into something coherent.

Maybe if we come across petty squabbles and misunderstandings in that journey, there is still time to end them. Time to realise that that's exactly what they were, petty and misunderstandings – not great feuds or coldnesses.

I said I would be honest in *LifeStory*, but you are free to gild things or rose tint them or soften sharp edges if you like.

But I hope it takes you on a good trip and that when you are finished you will know yourself and the world you have lived in much better.

To have helped the Irish Hospice Foundation *and* to have made a stab at the big cosmic questions like, 'What's it all about?' – that's a reward for buying this lovely book.

CREATING A GIFT OF MEMORIES

BY JOHN WATERS

FROM THE FIRST MARK
ON THE BLANK PAGE,
THIS BOOK WILL TAKE YOU
ON A UNIQUE JOURNEY
AND TELL A STORY LIKE
NO OTHER: YOUR STORY.

That is the message and meaning of *LifeStory*. The aim of this book is to help you excavate the detail of your life story and put it together in a coherent whole: the facts of your life, the history that went before, the significant locations of your own life and the life of your family and forebears, the visual record of those people and places that matter in your story.

We resemble and differ from one another in many ways. The sum of these resemblances and differences gives each of us our life story. For those we love and who love us, then, the most precious thing we can give them of ourselves is the detail, the fabric of that story. And the strange thing is that, in unearthing the story to make a gift for those we love, we are almost bound to find out things we barely knew about ourselves. These are some of the gifts this book promises you.

Sometimes, in our concentration on what our life is like now, we can miss the richness to be unearthed in the multiplicity of days behind us. The

different phases we have been through as human beings. The places where we have lived or been. The people we have known or become close to. The things that have happened to us, the significance of which only reveals itself with time. And, beyond that, the stories that led to our presence here in the first place: our antecedents and their hopes and dreams, their thoughts and deeds, their loves and losses.

This book is intended for everyone, young or old. It is for grown-ups to give to their children as a record of who they are, the story of their past lives, but also for children to begin creating their own stories from the other direction, the direction of the unfolding future. It is for lovers to exchange by way of betokening their love, or for friends to compare their memories of parallel journeys. Your story can be a solo project, but preferably it will be a collaboration with others whom you have loved and been loved by, those who can help you follow the threads of your past or your family's past, those whose memories of events is clearer or at least different to your own. Talk to your friends and family about what you're doing, and show them your work-in-progress in its varying stages of development. The more members of your family know what you're doing, the better your chances of getting pointed in the right direction. They may have stories or newspaper cuttings, photographs or other memorabilia to help you put the story together. It's amazing how a conversation can trigger a series of associations that will bring you quite literally back into a half-forgotten or half-remembered episode from your past. This is because, when someone is talking and describing things, we delve into our memories for images to give life to what they are saying. Older family members, like grandparents, are often delighted to be asked about the past, and very often they have information that even they have half forgotten because nobody has ever asked them about it. Ask friends of your parents or grandparents to tell you stories about their earlier lives. What was your mum like as a young woman? Did your dad chase girls on motorbikes, in absolute contradiction of his latter-day gravity? (Maybe he even had a motorbike of his own?)

Writing is an aid to remembering and not just a means of recording. Writing involves all the senses and can lead us into parts of ourselves that remain dormant at other times. It is especially good to write with a pen or pencil, rather than on a keyboard, because the physical act of writing in this way connects and activates the entire body and its sensory apparatus.

If you're right-handed, you might try writing with your left hand. Experts maintain that the non-dominant hand can be used to access forgotten parts of your experience. Because the experience of writing with your 'bad' hand brings back the experience of trying to write for the first time, it can trigger memories from deep in your childhood. Write down recollected conversations between yourself and other family members, using your two hands to lay down the two sides of the conversation.

Make use of photographs, and not just as illustrations for your story. Search through old family albums. Ask lots of questions about the photographs and the people in them. Look closely at the photographs of your parents and other family members. What is going on? What is the occasion and what are they feeling? Are there things about the photograph that seem odd to you today, perhaps the way people are dressed, or the way they stand or sit? Ask about it and write down what you think. If you

happen to be in the photograph, do you remember anything about the occasion? How did you feel that day? You may also wish to use video or audio recordings to tell parts of your story. Feel completely free.

You might try to find out about what was happening in the world at varying times in the history of your family. What was happening in the country when your parents first started going out together? Does your dad remember where he was the day John F. Kennedy or John Lennon was assassinated, the day Elvis Presley died? What was number one in the charts the day you were born? The Internet is an invaluable tool in this kind of research. As you proceed, you'll become more adept at turning up these details. You'll be amazed at how much remembering resembles things like playing tennis or learning to play the piano – the more you do it, the easier it'll get. As you go along, one memory will free up another. More and more will be revealed.

As you will see, the book is divided into sections to allow you to tackle different aspects of your story and to prompt you in varying directions in search of the important details pertaining to your own life. These are intended purely as a guide. Feel free to ignore any sections that don't interest or excite you, or to create new sections if you feel that, in compiling this record of yourself and your family, we may have overlooked something. This book gives you nudges and prods, points you in certain directions, directs your attention to areas that might prove rewarding of exploration. But there are no rules. Start at the end if you like and work backwards into the past. Skip over the sections that may seem too difficult or uninspiring. If you run out of steam in one section, move on to another.

You can always come back to the unfinished section later on, when other details of the narrative have fallen into place. This is *your* journey.

The beginning is often the hardest part. To help you get started, we have scattered throughout the book a selection of 'First Lines' from the life stories of noted writers and personalities from around the world, to let you see how others have met the challenge of that first blank page.

We have chosen longer passages from celebrated Irish memoirs which are relevant to each section of *LifeStory*. By showing you how various authors have created voices with which to tell their own stories, these passages might inspire you with regard to style, mood and atmosphere. How do they start? What facts and details are considered important? How is the story developed?

Don't feel you have to finish your life story all at once. Give yourself time to become enthused by doing small amounts of digging to start with. As your curiosity increases, you'll find you're spending more time thinking about and working on your story. Relax, there are no deadlines except the ones you set yourself. Don't worry about the chronology of things. That will resolve itself in the finished book. Focus on whatever areas you're most interested in. Memories will return in no particular order. Get them down as they come, rather than as they happened. But, if it helps you to work systematically from A to Z, then do just that.

You may feel, perhaps, that this book is too beautiful to write in. This is understandable. However, the more you write, the more beautiful the book will become. And don't feel that, because the book is so nice, everything you put in it must be flawless. It doesn't matter if you make mistakes. Cross

them out or, better still, leave them be. Mistakes are part of life too. Don't worry about grammar or spelling any more than you normally would, perhaps less. The more mistakes you make, the more of you will be in the book. Unless you're perfect, in which case the impeccable spelling and grammar will speak of who you truly are!

Use I, *me, we* or *us* as much as you like. That's the whole point. Be as specific as possible. Give names, dates, times, places. Give the names of your mum's favourite songs from her teenage years, rather than simply saying she was 'into pop music'. Don't be vague.

Memories can be deceptive. Sometimes what we 'remember' is what we have persuaded ourselves to be true by a process of self-deception or distortion. Sometimes our imaginations get mixed up with reality, so that what goes into the memory bank is a mixture of fact and fantasy. Sometimes, too, particularly as children, we confuse emotion with fact, remember things with great clarity because of the emotional events that occurred around them, while forgetting things that adults remember more easily because they didn't have any particular emotional significance. Check the facts. If there are different versions of the same event, why not get them all down?

Write about what you felt, what you saw, what you smelled, what you heard. Why not write an account of a day spent with each member of your family, using it to describe them and how you felt about them?

Write lists. What did your mum cook for dinner most days? Did your dad whistle or sing as he worked, and if so what? Can you remember the three best pieces of advice your grandfather ever gave you?

Another good technique is to allow your imagination to travel back in time to a place or point that you want to remember. It might be the house in which you grew up, a major event in your childhood or a first kiss. Lie down and close your eyes. Imagine yourself back in that time and place. Listen to the sounds around you. What do you hear? What do you smell? What did you feel like back then?

What about tracking down your family coat-of-arms? These days it's easy to do using the Internet. Do a search on one of the main search engines and if it exists you can probably find it in a few minutes. There are many fascinating things to be learned about the essential qualities and characteristics of your family by studying its coat-of-arms.

Most of all, have fun. This is not the National Library (although it's not impossible that your search for the past might bring you there). You don't have to whisper and tiptoe around. Laugh. Cry if you want. Get your tears of laughter or remembering to fall on the page.

The more of yourself you get onto these pages, the better this gift of memories, your *LifeStory*, will be.

It is always difficult to find a beginning. **It is with a kind of fear that I begin to write the history of my life.** I am consumed by memories and they form the life of me; stories that make up my life and lend it whatever veracity and purpose it may have. **Here is a memory.** My mother didn't try to stab my father until I was six, but she must have shown signs of oddness before that. **My father and mother should have stayed in New York where they met and married and where I was born.** I knew very little about my antecedents until I began writing this book. **At the age of fifteen my grandmother became the concubine of a warlord general, the police chief of a tenuous national government of China.** On 4 May 1923 I was born, but in giving me life my mother sacrificed her own. **I got my first lessons from my parents and, like most children, I learned the basic rules of survival and life-skills before my school years in Rush began at the age of five.** Early on the morning of August 19, 1946, I was born under a clear sky after a violent summer storm to a widowed mother in the Julia Chester Hospital in Hope, a town of about six thousand in south-west Arkansas, thirty-three miles east of the Texas border at Texarkana. **I sat cross-legged on the floor of the tiny home I'd created out of cardboard boxes.** When you're small you know nothing. **However long we may live, we never forget the time when we were young.** It started with the stuff of memory, which for me meant the four most enduring memories of my teen years. **My Mother was appalled at what I proposed to do – and not for the first time.** At the age of twenty I was released from an internment camp without money or job. **I cannot remember when these curious moments of suspense first began, when I would find myself unanchored and adrift in the dark, groping for clues as to where I was.** When I was about eight, or maybe nine, my friend Ron introduced me to a life of crime. **When you're a child, and you're poor, and you live next to other people who are poor, you never think of yourself as being poor.** Bono sidles up to me and gives me a great, big smile. **One of my earliest**

FAMILY STORY

IN THIS, THE OPENING PASSAGE FROM HIS AUTOBIOGRAPHY, *An Only Child*, FRANK O'CONNOR BEGINS HIS LIFE STORY BY SUMMONING UP THE STREET AND THE HOUSE WHERE HE GREW UP.

As a matter of historical fact I know that I was born in 1903 when we were living in Douglas Street, Cork, over a small sweet-and-tobacco shop kept by a middle-aged lady called Wall, but my memories have nothing to do with living in Douglas Street. My memories begin in Blarney Street, which we called Blarney Lane because it follows the track of an old lane from Cork to Blarney. It begins at the foot of Shandon Street, near the river-bank, in sordidness, and ascends the hill to something like squalor. No. 251, where we lived, is one of the cottages on the right near the top, though I realize now that it would be more properly described as a cabin, for it contained nothing but a tiny kitchen and a tiny bedroom with a loft above it. For this we paid two and sixpence – sixty cents – a week.

– Frank O'Connor, *An Only Child*

WHAT CAN YOU DISCOVER ABOUT . . .

WHERE YOUR FAMILY
CAME FROM?

HOW YOUR FAMILY SURVIVED
VARIOUS HISTORICAL EVENTS?

FAMILY LEGENDS?

ANY FAMOUS ANCESTORS?

WHAT YOUR GREAT-GRANDPARENTS
WERE LIKE?

ANY FAMILY FORTUNES WON OR LOST?

ANY FAMILY TRAGEDIES OR
SCANDALS?

WHAT YOUR ANCESTORS DID?

HOW YOUR PARENTS MET?

ANY FOREIGN RELATIONS?

YOUR FAMILY NAMES?

FIRST LINES

It is always difficult to find a beginning.

FROM *An Evil Cradling* BY BRIAN KEENAN FIRST PUBLISHED BY HUTCHINSON LONDON, 1992

It is with a kind of fear that I begin to write the history of my life.

FROM *The Story of My Life*
BY HELEN KELLER
PUBLISHED BY
HODDER AND STOUGHTON
LONDON, 1970

FIRST LINES

I am consumed by memories and they form the life of me; stories that make up my life and lend it whatever veracity and purpose it may have.

FROM *Donkey's Years*
BY AIDAN HIGGINS
FIRST PUBLISHED BY
MARTIN SECKER & WARBURG
LONDON, 1995

FIRST LINES

Here is a memory.

From *All of These People*
by Fergal Keane
First published by
HaperCollins Publishers
London, 2005

FIRST LINES

My mother didn't try to stab my father until I was six, but she must have shown signs of oddness before that.

FROM *Never Have Your Dog Stuffed*
BY ALAN ALDA
FIRST PUBLISHED BY
RANDOM HOUSE
NEW YORK, 2006

memories is of a little boy hanging out of the second-floor window of a house overlooking the Square in Mountmellick, County Laois. Frank Lahiffe loved Mary O'Dwyer as well. Dylan told me that he loved me the very first night we met, and although I had made love before, this was something that no other man had ever said to me. Mike and I were childhood sweethearts. Most of my adult life has been spent loving one man. In the summer of 1967, when I was ten years old, my father caved in to my persistent pleas and took me to get my own dog. A slight sound woke me, and when I opened my eyes, I was staring into the face of a lion. Ní rabhas mórán thar dhá bhliain go leith i Londain Shasana an tráth úd, ach mar sin féin, ní mórán achair eile a d'fhanfainn ann dá mbeadh – sea, caithfear a rá – dá mbeadh an oiread agam is a bhéarfadh abhaile mé. The soil in Leitrim is poor, in places no more than an inch deep. How to sort out one's confused love-hate relationship with the place that gave one birth? I remember the strange humidity during that first September in the city. On my tenth birthday, a bicycle and an atlas coincided as presents and a few days later I decided to cycle to India. One month after I had started my journey around the circumference of America, I was back again where I began, on the frantic concourse at Penn Station, in Madison Square Gardens, New York — I hate neat endings. They say flying can do strange things to your mind, and an aeroplane is not the best place to commit thoughts to paper, but what the hell: this little diary of a year in the life of a professional rugby player has to start somewhere, and cruising at 550 mph at 37,000 feet with my feet up seems as good a place as any. The school was new, like everything around us. There is no doubt but youth is a fine thing though my own is not over yet and wisdom comes with age. 'All advice is perfectly useless,' my father told me when he sent me away to school. At the time of my father's execution and of the 1916 Rising, I was at school in Paris. In Alsace, round about 1850, a schoolmaster, burdened with children, agreed to become a grocer. I

PORTRAITS

IN THIS EXTRACT FROM HIS MEMOIR, *In the Dark Room,* BRIAN DILLON PUZZLES OVER A PHOTOGRAPH OF HIS PARENTS AS A YOUNG COUPLE WALKING ACROSS DUBLIN'S O'CONNELL BRIDGE.

The photograph intrigues and appals me for this reason: it may be that I would never have existed but for this night, but, perhaps, for this very moment. Could it be that my parents do not yet know each other well? Is this not only the first photographic evidence I have of their relationship but – and the thought sends me back to the image, plunged now in a sort of vertigo, stranded on the bridge between actuality and a past without me – the very first photograph of them together? If so, it may be that the moment they were accosted by the photographer (I imagine my father gallantly, awkwardly amused, giving his name and address) was the very moment they began to consider themselves a couple. In the flash which isolates them, happily illumined against the black ground, the photographer fails to record that I am waiting in the darkness. The photo is part of me, though I can't recall it. My memory depends on this black hole in time, an unknowable moment at which the collection comes together, becomes the record of another sort of memory: that of my family.

– Brian Dillon, *In the Dark Room*

WHAT DO YOU REMEMBER ABOUT . . .

YOUR FAVOURITE AUNT OR UNCLE?

THE BLACK SHEEP OF THE FAMILY?

THE STORY BEHIND A FAMILY
PHOTOGRAPH?

A SPECIAL MOMENT WITH YOUR
MUM OR DAD?

A COLOURFUL COUSIN?

ANY SOLDIERS IN THE FAMILY?

RELATIVES YOU WERE AFRAID OF?

FAMOUS FAMILY ROWS?

THE FAMILY MEMBER YOU ARE
MOST LIKE?

A BROTHER OR SISTER BEING BORN?

SIBLING RIVALRY?

A FOSTER BROTHER OR SISTER?

THE FAMILY COMEDIAN?

AN EMBARRASSING FAMILY MOMENT?

A FAMILY ECCENTRIC?

OUTLAWED IN-LAWS?

FIRST LINES

My father and mother
should have stayed in
New York where they met
and married and where
I was born.

FROM *Angela's Ashes*
BY FRANK MCCOURT
FIRST PUBLISHED BY
SCRIBNER
NEW YORK, 1996

I knew very little about
my antecedents until
I began writing this book.

FROM *John Major, the Autobiography*
BY JOHN MAJOR
FIRST PUBLISHED BY
HARPERCOLLINS PUBLISHERS
LONDON, 1999

FIRST LINES

At the age of fifteen my grandmother became the concubine of a warlord general, the police chief of a tenuous national government of China.

FROM *Wild Swans*
BY JUNG CHANG
FIRST PUBLISHED BY
HARPERCOLLINS PUBLISHERS
LONDON, 1991

FIRST LINES

On 4 May 1923 I was born, but in giving me life my mother sacrificed her own.

FROM *If I Don't Write It, Nobody Else Will*
BY ERIC SYKES
FIRST PUBLISHED BY
FOURTH ESTATE
LONDON, 2005

wasn't born a First Lady or a Senator. During the summer, I recorded an interview for TG4 and one of the questions I was asked sparked a trail of thought that forced me to view my life from the outside, looking in. A friend of my father's would counter any perceived crises in his working life by saying: 'we are only passing through.' It was my birthday but the white-water rafting was shut. A few months before starting to write this book, I celebrated my sixtieth birthday. They take you back, those hymns, those chanted psalms, those supremely confident words sung to graceful music. I am Patrick, a sinner, the most unlearned of men, the lowliest of all the faithful, utterly worthless in the eyes of many. I was born on March 2nd, 1921, into an observant, Jewish, middle-class family in Bratislava, then part of Czechoslovakia. It's in there all the time, looking for a way out. I was always determined to make my mark in this wonderful yet often so weird game of football. I was lying in my sleeping bag, staring at the light filtering through the red and green fabric of the dome tent. The Gaelic Athletic Association had no presence on the island where I grew up. Lou Levy, top man of Leeds Music Publishing company, took me up in a taxi to the Pythian Temple on West 70th Street to show me the pocket sized recording studio where Bill Haley and His Comets had recorded "Rock Around the Clock" — then down to Jack Dempsey's restaurant on 58th and Broadway, where we sat down in a red leather upholstered booth facing the front window. This is the year that I'm going to become horticulturally correct. The year began with lunch. The first thing I remember is the gramophone arriving. I fled Tibet on 31 March 1959. The morning of May 10, 1940, was fine all over Europe. My love for Northern Ireland and the people who inhabit our community has been the underlying theme of my whole life. When the idea first came up that I should let my name stand for president of Czechoslovakia, it seemed like an absurd joke. At four o' clock in the afternoon of Thursday 24 October 1963, I was in Rome, in my room at the Hotel Minerva; I was to fly home the

EARLY YEARS

IN THIS PASSAGE FROM *Memoir*, JOHN MCGAHERN REMEMBERS THE ARRIVAL OF HIS FIRST SIBLINGS AND AN EARLY ATTEMPT HE MADE TO DO THEM IN.

I was a single star until the twins arrived, and I became insanely jealous of the natural transfer of attention. On dry days, when my mother was at school, my grandmother often left the twins out in the sun between the house and the forge, high on the sloping pass of clinkers that ran to the open gate on the road. I was forever around the forge, and she would warn me to mind them before going back into the house, having locked the brake on their big pram. I must have been planning how to get them out of my life for some time. I learned to unlock the brake, and one day, after careful checking that nobody was watching either from the forge or the house or the road, I pushed the pram down the slope. The pass wasn't steep and the wheels would have bumped and slowed on the clinkers, but before it came to a stop the pram wheeled off the pass and overturned. The twins weren't hurt, but all this time my grandmother had been observing me from behind a curtain, and made not the slightest attempt – she had only to tap the window – to protect the twins, though she was out of the house and able to seize me as I was watching the pram overturn in terrified dismay.

– John McGahern, *Memoir*

WHAT CAN YOU WRITE ABOUT. . .

YOUR EARLIEST MEMORY?

THE SONG THAT WAS NUMBER ONE
WHEN YOU WERE BORN?

A SIGNIFICANT WORLD EVENT
IN THE NEWSPAPER HEADLINES ON
THE DAY YOU WERE BORN?

THE GAMES YOU PLAYED?

THOSE DREADED PIANO LESSONS?

WHAT YOU SANG IN THE SCHOOL
CONCERT?

YOUR FAVOURITE BEDTIME STORY?

THE FIRST BOOK WITHOUT PICTURES
THAT YOU EVER READ?

ILLNESSES, BROKEN BONES OR
OPERATIONS?

A NEIGHBOURHOOD BULLY?

POCKET MONEY?

HOUSEHOLD CHORES YOU HAD TO DO?

A NICKNAME YOU REALLY DISLIKED?

FIRST LINES

I got my first lessons from my parents and, like most children, I learned the basic rules of survival and life-skills before my school years in Rush began at the age of five.

FROM *Sand In My Shoes*
BY NIALL WELDON
FIRST PUBLISHED BY
ASHFIELD PRESS
DUBLIN, 2005

Early on the morning of August 19, 1946, I was born under a clear sky after a violent summer storm to a widowed mother in the Julia Chester Hospital in Hope, a town of about six thousand in south-west Arkansas, thirty-three miles east of the Texas border at Texarkana.

FROM *My Life*
BY BILL CLINTON
FIRST PUBLISHED BY
RANDOM HOUSE
NEW YORK, 2004

FIRST LINES

I sat cross-legged on the floor of the tiny home I'd created out of cardboard boxes.

FROM *My Life So Far*
BY JANE FONDA
FIRST PUBLISHED BY
RANDOM HOUSE
NEW YORK, 2005

next day and I was putting papers away when the telephone rang. In the mid-1950s, when I was fourteen or fifteen, I told my mother I was homosexual: that was the word, back then, *homosexual*, in its full satanic majesty, cloaked in ether fumes, a combination of evil and sickness. Caron and I never talked about death – only about life. A few months after the accident I had an idea for a short film about a quadriplegic who lives in a dream. Long, long before I came to know and love Africa as a place, I yearned for it as an idea. In the fall of 1995, after resigning from my last academic post, I decided to indulge myself and fulfill a dream. I tried to hide the secrets of my past from my wife for as long as I could. Deir siad go bhfuil an fhírinne searbh, ach, creid mise ní searbh atá sí ach garbh, agus sin an fáth a seachantar í. I hope I will be able to confide everything to you, as I have never been able to confide in anyone, and I hope you will be a great source of comfort and support. On the floor in a corner of my study, sticking out from under a pile of other papers, is a shabby old green folder containing a manuscript I believe will tell me a lot about my family and my own past. It is always difficult to find a beginning. It is with a kind of fear that I begin to write the history of my life. I am consumed by memories and they form the life of me; stories that make up my life and lend it whatever veracity and purpose it may have. Here is a memory. My mother didn't try to stab my father until I was six, but she must have shown signs of oddness before that. My father and mother should have stayed in New York where they met and married and where I was born. I knew very little about my antecedents until I began writing this book. At the age of fifteen my grandmother became the concubine of a warlord general, the police chief of a tenuous national government of China. On 4 May 1923 I was born, but in giving me life my mother sacrificed her own. I got my first lessons from my parents and, like most children, I learned the basic rules of survival and life-skills before my school years in Rush began at the age of five. Early on the morning of

GROWING UP

IN THIS PASSAGE FROM *Vive Moi!*, ONE OF TWO MEMOIRS BY SEAN O'FAOLAIN, THE AUTHOR RECALLS SOME BITTERSWEET MEMORIES OF EARLY SCHOOLDAYS.

Besides, my body also held out. I was in that swoon of puberty that I have described when recalling my last visit to my Kildare cousins in the military camp on the Curragh, a boy doubly lost, to the objective world of action, in the subjective world of sexual desire, free of neither city, longing for the freedom of both. If only the outer world could be filled again, as it had been before, I might have struck a balance. I was aware only of my own emptiness and my body's frets. Was this the time in me that made that good brother say of me, 'A nice lad, but . . .' and tap his head? How can I tell, since these were years to which, as I have described, my memory is a near blank? Yet, not a total blank; I was not all that dotty. I remember the day I, without realising it, began to see light through a tiny circle.

– Sean O'Faolain, *Vive Moi!*

Were you . . .

A DIFFICULT OR AN EASY TEENAGER?

FULL OF SELF-DOUBT OR
BRIMMING WITH CONFIDENCE?

ALWAYS ROWING WITH YOUR
PARENTS?

A DABBLER IN DRINK OR DRUGS?

VERY TRENDY? (DESCRIBE THAT
FAVOURITE OUTFIT – JUST HOW BAD
WAS IT?)

A TEDDY BOY, A HIPPIE, A GOTH,
OR, ADMIT IT, A NERD?

THE HEART-THROB OF YOUR
NEIGHBOURHOOD?

ALWAYS DECORATING YOUR
BEDROOM?

ALLOWED TO GO TO DANCES
OR MUSIC FESTIVALS?

FIRST LINES

When you're small you know nothing.

FROM *The Speckled People*
BY HUGO HAMILTON
FIRST PUBLISHED BY
FOURTH ESTATE
LONDON, 2003

However long we may live, we never forget the time when we were young.

FROM *Pelé, the Autobiography*
BY PELÉ
WITH ORLANDO DUARTE AND
ALEX BELLOS
FIRST PUBLISHED BY
SIMON & SCHUSTER UK
LONDON, 2006

It started with the stuff
of memory, which for me
meant the four most
enduring memories of my
teen years.

FROM *Oughtobiography*
BY DAVID MARCUS
FIRST PUBLISHED BY
GILL & MACMILLAN
DUBLIN, 2001

August 19, 1946, I was born under a clear sky after a violent summer storm to a widowed mother in the Julia Chester Hospital in Hope, a town of about six thousand in south-west Arkansas, thirty-three miles east of the Texas border at Texarkana. I sat cross-legged on the floor of the tiny home I'd created out of cardboard boxes. When you're small you know nothing. However long we may live, we never forget the time when we were young. It started with the stuff of memory, which for me meant the four most enduring memories of my teen years. My Mother was appalled at what I proposed to do – and not for the first time. At the age of twenty I was released from an internment camp without money or job. I cannot remember when these curious moments of suspense first began, when I would find myself unanchored and adrift in the dark, groping for clues as to where I was. When I was about eight, or maybe nine, my friend Ron introduced me to a life of crime. When you're a child, and you're poor, and you live next to other people who are poor, you never think of yourself as being poor. Bono sidles up to me and gives me a great, big smile. One of my earliest memories is of a little boy hanging out of the second-floor window of a house overlooking the Square in Mountmellick, County Laois. Frank Lahiffe loved Mary O'Dwyer as well. Dylan told me that he loved me the very first night we met, and although I had made love before, this was something that no other man had ever said to me. Mike and I were childhood sweethearts. Most of my adult life has been spent loving one man. In the summer of 1967, when I was ten years old, my father caved in to my persistent pleas and took me to get my own dog. A slight sound woke me, and when I opened my eyes, I was staring into the face of a lion. Ní rabhas mórán thar dhá bhliain go leith i Londain Shasana an tráth úd, ach mar sin féin, ní mórán achair eile a d'fhanfainn ann dá mbeadh – sea, caithfear a rá – dá mbeadh an oiread agam is a bhéarfadh abhaile mé. The soil in Leitrim is poor, in places no more than an inch deep. How to sort out one's confused love-hate relationship

LEAVING

In *An Evil Cradling*, THE STORY OF HIS ABDUCTION AND IMPRISONMENT IN LEBANON, BRIAN KEENAN RECALLS HIS PREPARATIONS FOR LEAVING BELFAST.

In the days before catching the flight I spent some time traipsing around the old haunts of Belfast, talking with friends about my plans and what the future might hold for me. But most of those last few days I spent alone.

I suppose I had to take a parting look at the place I was leaving. I remember driving or walking around the back streets of the areas in which I had worked with different community groups. I particularly remember those stark murals, colourful and grotesque, which have come to be part of Belfast, and part of the historic expression of the people and their city. A great lumbering white horse and small rider painted obscurely on a gable wall of some tiny side street: this Dutch king in a foreign land, taking different form and shape from the hands of the naive painters. And always there was that Viking bloody red hand, the symbol of Protestant Ulster.

In the Catholic areas the murals reversed out of a black background. I remember somewhere a crude copy of Michelangelo's *Pietá*, painted against a backdrop of men with Armalites: raised, defiant, clenched fists which declared more rage against God and man, I thought, than any conformity with the politics of nationalism.

– Brian Keenan, *An Evil Cradling*

WHEN YOU FIRST LEFT HOME . . .

DID YOU LEAVE FOR GOOD?

WAS IT TO LOOK FOR WORK?

WERE YOUR PARENTS UPSET?

WERE YOU ENCOURAGED TO GO?

WAS THERE A SEND-OFF?

WERE YOU NERVOUS?

WAS IT TO GO AWAY TO STUDY?

WAS IT TO GET MARRIED?

WERE YOU EMIGRATING?

WAS IT TO JOIN THE ARMY?

DID YOU LEAVE BY BUS, TRAIN,
CAR OR PLANE?

WHAT WAS IN YOUR SUITCASE?

DID YOU TAKE A MEMENTO
FROM HOME?

HOW LONG WAS IT BEFORE YOU
RETURNED?

My Mother was appalled
at what I proposed to
do – and not for the first
time.

FROM *In the Firing Line*
BY BRIAN MAWHINNEY
FIRST PUBLISHED BY
HARPERCOLLINS PUBLISHERS
LONDON, 1999

FIRST LINES

At the age of twenty
I was released from an
internment camp without
money or job.

FROM *My Father's Son*
BY FRANK O'CONNOR
FIRST PUBLISHED BY
MACMILLAN & CO
LONDON, 1968

FIRST LINES

I cannot remember when these curious moments of suspense first began, when I would find myself unanchored and adrift in the dark, groping for clues as to where I was.

FROM *Point of Departure*
BY JAMES CAMERON
FIRST PUBLISHED BY
ARTHUR BARKER
LONDON, 1967

with the place that gave one birth? I remember the strange humidity during that first September in the city. On my tenth birthday, a bicycle and an atlas coincided as presents and a few days later I decided to cycle to India. One month after I had started my journey around the circumference of America, I was back again where I began, on the frantic concourse at Penn Station, in Madison Square Gardens, New York — I hate neat endings. They say flying can do strange things to your mind, and an aeroplane is not the best place to commit thoughts to paper, but what the hell: this little diary of a year in the life of a professional rugby player has to start somewhere, and cruising at 550 mph at 37,000 feet with my feet up seems as good a place as any. The school was new, like everything around us. There is no doubt but youth is a fine thing though my own is not over yet and wisdom comes with age. 'All advice is perfectly useless,' my father told me when he sent me away to school. At the time of my father's execution and of the 1916 Rising, I was at school in Paris. In Alsace, round about 1850, a schoolmaster, burdened with children, agreed to become a grocer. I wasn't born a First Lady or a Senator. During the summer, I recorded an interview for TG4 and one of the questions I was asked sparked a trail of thought that forced me to view my life from the outside, looking in. A friend of my father's would counter any perceived crises in his working life by saying: 'we are only passing through.' It was my birthday but the white-water rafting was shut. A few months before starting to write this book, I celebrated my sixtieth birthday. They take you back, those hymns, those chanted psalms, those supremely confident words sung to graceful music. I am Patrick, a sinner, the most unlearned of men, the lowliest of all the faithful, utterly worthless in the eyes of many. I was born on March 2nd, 1921, into an observant, Jewish, middle-class family in Bratislava, then part of Czechoslovakia. It's in there all the time, looking for a way out. I was always determined to make my mark in this wonderful yet often so weird game of football. I was lying in

FRIENDS

IN HIS MEMOIR, *The Rocky Years,*
FERDIA MAC ANNA CALLS TO MIND
A CHILDHOOD FRIEND WHO HAD
VANISHED FROM HIS LIFE.

My best friend in Killiney was Peter Green, who lived nearby. We played together most days. I was four when our family left the house in Killiney to move into an apartment in the city, though Mother promised that she'd bring me back every weekend to play with Peter – but she never did and I never saw him again. Perhaps she meant to bring me back to Killiney to play with my friend, but forgot. Maybe it was just a promise made to smooth over the moment of departure, but I couldn't understand why Peter had suddenly disappeared from my world. I couldn't understand why my parents couldn't fix the problem. I felt a terrible sense of loss, made worse because it was unexplained.

Many years later I moved back to the southside, to a house less than a mile from our first home in Killiney. Once, when she was visiting, Mother claimed to have met Peter's mother. Peter was a merchant navigator at sea. Apparently he still remembered me and for a long time after I left expected me to return to play with him at weekends.

– Ferdia Mac Anna, *The Rocky Years*

WHY NOT WRITE ABOUT. . .

HOW YOU MET YOUR BEST FRIEND?

THE GAMES YOU PLAYED?

HOW OFTEN YOU FOUGHT AND
THEN MADE UP?

PRANKS YOU PLAYED TOGETHER?

A TIME YOU GOT INTO TROUBLE?

YOUR OLD GANG?

YOUR BEST FRIEND NOW?

EXPERIENCES SHARED WITH FRIENDS?

WORK FRIENDS?

SPORTING PALS?

THE BEST TIMES YOU HAD TOGETHER?

A TIME WHEN A FRIEND
SUPPORTED YOU?

THAT FRIEND FROM THE PAST
YOU HAVEN'T SEEN FOR YEARS?

YOUR OLDEST FRIEND?

When I was about eight, or maybe nine, my friend Ron introduced me to a life of crime.

FROM *And Why Not?*
BY BARRY NORMAN
FIRST PUBLISHED BY
SIMON & SCHUSTER UK
LONDON, 2002

When you're a child, and you're poor, and you live next to other people who are poor, you never think of yourself as being poor.

FROM *Time Added On*
BY GEORGE HOOK
FIRST PUBLISHED BY
PENGUIN IRELAND
DUBLIN, 2005

FIRST LINES

Bono sidles up to me and gives me a great, big smile.

FROM *On the Road*
BY SHAY HEALY
FIRST PUBLISHED BY
THE O'BRIEN PRESS
DUBLIN, 2005

FIRST LINES

One of my earliest
memories is of a little boy
hanging out of the
second-floor window of
a house overlooking the
Square in Mountmellick,
County Laois.

FROM *Hurler on the Ditch*
BY MICHAEL MILLS
FIRST PUBLISHED BY
CURRACH PRESS
DUBLIN, 2005

my sleeping bag, staring at the light filtering through the red and green fabric of the dome tent. **The Gaelic Athletic Association had no presence on the island where I grew up.** Lou Levy, top man of Leeds Music Publishing company, took me up in a taxi to the Pythian Temple on West 70th Street to show me the pocket sized recording studio where Bill Haley and His Comets had recorded "Rock Around the Clock" — then down to Jack Dempsey's restaurant on 58th and Broadway, where we sat down in a red leather upholstered booth facing the front window. **This is the year that I'm going to become horticulturally correct.** The year began with lunch. **The first thing I remember is the gramophone arriving.** I fled Tibet on 31 March 1959. **The morning of May 10, 1940, was fine all over Europe.** My love for Northern Ireland and the people who inhabit our community has been the underlying theme of my whole life. **When the idea first came up that I should let my name stand for president of Czechoslovakia, it seemed like an absurd joke.** At four o' clock in the afternoon of Thursday 24 October 1963, I was in Rome, in my room at the Hotel Minerva; I was to fly home the next day and I was putting papers away when the telephone rang. **In the mid-1950s, when I was fourteen or fifteen, I told my mother I was homosexual: that was the word, back then, *homosexual*, in its full satanic majesty, cloaked in ether fumes, a combination of evil and sickness.** Caron and I never talked about death — only about life. **A few months after the accident I had an idea for a short film about a quadriplegic who lives in a dream.** Long, long before I came to know and love Africa as a place, I yearned for it as an idea. **In the fall of 1995, after resigning from my last academic post, I decided to indulge myself and fulfill a dream.** I tried to hide the secrets of my past from my wife for as long as I could. **Deir siad go bhfuil an fhírinne searbh, ach, creid mise ní searbh atá sí ach garbh, agus sin an fáth a seachantar í.** I hope I will be able to confide everything to you, as I have never been able to confide in anyone, and I hope you will be a great source of comfort and

LOVES

In this extract from *Follow Your Dream*, Daniel O'Donnell reflects on the heartaches of romance and remembers his first love.

Cupid has a lot to answer for. The palpitations you experience whenever you set eyes on the object of your desires. The butterflies in your tummy that kill your appetite and make your mother think you're ailing, and should she call a doctor? The all-consuming passion in the first flush of love that makes you lose interest in everything else. Cupid must have a great laugh, watching the effects of that little arrow.

The first love of my life came along when I was only a wee lad in national school. A little girl arrived in our area on holidays, and, God, she was the most beautiful little girl I had ever laid eyes on. I suppose I was curious about her because she was a stranger. She was exotic to me because she came from the outside. To this day, I don't even know what part of the country or the world she was from. At secondary school, there were also a couple of girls with whom I had a brief and innocent attachment. I was always very secretive about them because I didn't want my mother to know. I probably felt that she would frown on me getting involved with a girl at that early stage of my life and try to put a stop to it.

– Daniel O'Donnell, *Follow Your Dream*

When you close your eyes,
what can you recall about . . .

THE LOVE OF YOUR LIFE?

A FIRST ROMANCE?

LOVE AT FIRST SIGHT?

YOUR FIRST KISS?

THE PAIN OF YOUR FIRST BREAK-UP?

THE PEOPLE WHO LOVED YOU
MORE THAN YOU LOVED THEM?

REGRETS ABOUT LOST LOVE?

PLACES YOU ASSOCIATE WITH LOVE?

UNREQUITED LOVE?

SONGS THAT MAKE YOUR HEART
FLUTTER?

MEETING YOUR SPOUSE OR PARTNER?

DIFFICULT TIMES YOU ENDURED
TOGETHER?

BEST TIMES TOGETHER – SO FAR?

Frank Lahiffe loved
Mary O'Dwyer as well.

FROM *Is That It?*
BY BOB GELDOF
FIRST PUBLISHED BY
SIDGWICK & JACKSON
LONDON, 1986

FIRST LINES

Dylan told me that he loved me the very first night we met, and although I had made love before, this was something that no other man had ever said to me.

FROM *A Warring Absence*
BY CAITLIN THOMAS
SECKER & WARBURG
LONDON, 1986

FIRST LINES

Mike and I were
childhood sweethearts.

From *A Mother's Story*
by Sara Payne
First published by
Hodder and Stoughton
London, 2004

FIRST LINES

Most of my adult life
has been spent loving
one man.

FROM *Loving George*
BY ALEX BEST
FIRST PUBLISHED BY
JOHN BLAKE PUBLISHING
LONDON, 2006

support. On the floor in a corner of my study, sticking out from under a pile of other papers, is a shabby old green folder containing a manuscript I believe will tell me a lot about my family and my own past. It is always difficult to find a beginning. It is with a kind of fear that I begin to write the history of my life. I am consumed by memories and they form the life of me; stories that make up my life and lend it whatever veracity and purpose it may have. Here is a memory. My mother didn't try to stab my father until I was six, but she must have shown signs of oddness before that. My father and mother should have stayed in New York where they met and married and where I was born. I knew very little about my antecedents until I began writing this book. At the age of fifteen my grandmother became the concubine of a warlord general, the police chief of a tenuous national government of China. On 4 May 1923 I was born, but in giving me life my mother sacrificed her own. I got my first lessons from my parents and, like most children, I learned the basic rules of survival and life-skills before my school years in Rush began at the age of five. Early on the morning of August 19, 1946, I was born under a clear sky after a violent summer storm to a widowed mother in the Julia Chester Hospital in Hope, a town of about six thousand in south-west Arkansas, thirty-three miles east of the Texas border at Texarkana. I sat cross-legged on the floor of the tiny home I'd created out of cardboard boxes. When you're small you know nothing. However long we may live, we never forget the time when we were young. It started with the stuff of memory, which for me meant the four most enduring memories of my teen years. My Mother was appalled at what I proposed to do – and not for the first time. At the age of twenty I was released from an internment camp without money or job. I cannot remember when these curious moments of suspense first began, when I would find myself unanchored and adrift in the dark, groping for clues as to where I was. When I was about eight, or maybe nine, my friend Ron introduced me to a life of crime. When

ANIMALS

IN HER FIRST MEMOIR, *To School Through the Fields*, ALICE TAYLOR REMEMBERS SOME OF THE FARM ANIMALS THAT POPULATED HER CHILDHOOD.

Of all the animals that belonged on the farm, it was Paddy's death that caused most trauma in our house. He was older than I and was a horse with great class. In animals you get as much individual variation as in humans: there are the mean, sly, stupid, intelligent and honest ones just the same as us. Paddy was the cream of the animal world. He would neither kick nor bite and was hard-working. He was also an honest animal – if you think there is no such thing as a dishonest animal then you have never heard of a thieving cow. Some cows always have their heads up to see if there is something better in the next field and if there is, up and over they go to get it. We have that much in common with the cows. With horses, when they worked in pairs there was the one who pulled hardest and did the most work; there was also the horse who had no mean traits and was loved and respected by his owner. Such a horse was Paddy.

– Alice Taylor, *To School Through the Fields*

WHAT MEMORIES DO YOU HAVE OF . . .

YOUR FIRST PET?

ANIMALS WITH PERSONALITY?

THE ANIMAL YOU LOVED MOST
AS A CHILD?

PETS SLEEPING IN YOUR ROOM?

A PET RUNNING AWAY?

CARING FOR AN ANIMAL?

TRAINING DIFFICULT PETS?

EMERGENCY VISITS TO THE VET?

A PET THAT HAD TO BE PUT TO SLEEP?

TRICKS THEY LEARNED?

ANIMALS BEING BORN?

A BAD ENCOUNTER WITH AN ANIMAL?

SEEING A WILD ANIMAL FOR
THE FIRST TIME?

MILKING A COW?

GOING TO THE ZOO?

FIRST LINES

In the summer of 1967, when I was ten years old, my father caved in to my persistent pleas and took me to get my own dog.

FROM *Marley & Me*
BY JOHN GROGAN
FIRST PUBLISHED BY
HARPERCOLLINS PUBLISHERS
NEW YORK, 2005

FIRST LINES

A slight sound woke me, and when I opened my eyes, I was staring into the face of a lion.

FROM *Desert Flower*
BY WARIS DIRIE
FIRST PUBLISHED BY
WILLIAM MORROW & CO.
NEW YORK, 1998

you're a child, and you're poor, and you live next to other people who are poor, you never think of yourself as being poor. Bono sidles up to me and gives me a great, big smile. One of my earliest memories is of a little boy hanging out of the second-floor window of a house overlooking the Square in Mountmellick, County Laois. Frank Lahiffe loved Mary O'Dwyer as well. Dylan told me that he loved me the very first night we met, and although I had made love before, this was something that no other man had ever said to me. Mike and I were childhood sweethearts. Most of my adult life has been spent loving one man. In the summer of 1967, when I was ten years old, my father caved in to my persistent pleas and took me to get my own dog. A slight sound woke me, and when I opened my eyes, I was staring into the face of a lion. Ní rabhas mórán thar dhá bhliain go leith i Londain Shasana an tráth úd, ach mar sin féin, ní mórán achair eile a d'fhanfainn ann dá mbeadh – sea, caithfear a rá – dá mbeadh an oiread agam is a bhéarfadh abhaile mé. The soil in Leitrim is poor, in places no more than an inch deep. How to sort out one's confused love-hate relationship with the place that gave one birth? I remember the strange humidity during that first September in the city. On my tenth birthday, a bicycle and an atlas coincided as presents and a few days later I decided to cycle to India. One month after I had started my journey around the circumference of America, I was back again where I began, on the frantic concourse at Penn Station, in Madison Square Gardens, New York — I hate neat endings. They say flying can do strange things to your mind, and an aeroplane is not the best place to commit thoughts to paper, but what the hell: this little diary of a year in the life of a professional rugby player has to start somewhere, and cruising at 550 mph at 37,000 feet with my feet up seems as good a place as any. The school was new, like everything around us. There is no doubt but youth is a fine thing though my own is not over yet and wisdom comes with age. 'All advice is perfectly useless,' my father told me when he sent me away

PLACES

In *Angela's Ashes*, FRANK MCCOURT REMEMBERS HIS FAMILY MOVING UPSTAIRS TO ESCAPE A FLOOD AND THE POPE'S STERN GAZE.

Two weeks before Christmas Malachy and I come home from school in a heavy rain and when we push in the door we find the kitchen empty. The table and chairs and trunk are gone and the fire is dead in the grate. The Pope is still there and that means we haven't moved again. Dad would never move without the Pope. The kitchen floor is wet, little pools of water all around, and the walls are twinkling with the damp. There's a noise upstairs and when we go up we find Dad and Mam and the missing furniture. It's nice and warm there with a fire blazing in the grate, Mam sitting in the bed, and Dad reading *The Irish Press* and smoking a cigarette by the fire. Mam tells us there was a terrible flood, that the rain came down the lane and poured in under our door. They tried to stop it with rags but they only turned sopping wet and let the rain in. People emptying their buckets made it worse and there was a sickening stink in the kitchen. She thinks we should stay upstairs as long as there is rain. We'll be warm through the winter months and then we can go downstairs in the springtime if there is any sign of a dryness in the walls or the floor. Dad says it's like going away on our holidays to a warm foreign place like Italy. That's what we'll call the upstairs from now on, Italy.

– Frank McCourt, *Angela's Ashes*

Did you . . .

COME FROM A TOWN OR
THE COUNTRY?

EVER MOVE HOUSE?

GO BACK TO THE PLACE YOU
WERE BORN IN?

LIVE ABROAD AT ANY TIME?

HAVE A FAVOURITE ROOM IN
THE HOUSE?

HAVE A FAVOURITE CAFÉ OR PUB?

GO TO THE SEASIDE AS A CHILD?

EVER CLIMB A MOUNTAIN, BUILD
A TREE HOUSE OR GO FISHING?

HAVE A 'SECRET GARDEN'?

LIVE IN AN APARTMENT?

EVER GO BACK HOME TO RELIVE
A CHILDHOOD MEMORY?

EVER SLEEP IN A CARAVAN?

FIRST LINES

Ní rabhas mórán thar dhá bhliain go leith i Londain Shasana an tráth úd, ach mar sin féin, ní mórán achair eile a d'fhanfainn ann dá mbeadh – sea, caithfear a rá – dá mbeadh an oiread agam is a bhéarfadh abhaile mé.

As *Deoraíocht*
LE PÁDRAIC Ó CONAIRE
AN COMHLACHT OIDEACHAIS
BAILE ÁTHA CLIATH, 1994

FIRST LINES

The soil in Leitrim is poor, in places no more than an inch deep.

FROM *Memoir*
BY JOHN MCGAHERN
FIRST PUBLISHED BY
FABER AND FABER
LONDON, 2005

FIRST LINES

How to sort out one's confused love-hate relationship with the place that gave one birth?

FROM *Bonfires on the Hillside*
BY JAMES KELLY
FIRST PUBLISHED BY
FOUNTAIN PUBLISHING
BELFAST, 1995

to school. At the time of my father's execution and of the 1916 Rising, I was at school in Paris. In Alsace, round about 1850, a schoolmaster, burdened with children, agreed to become a grocer. I wasn't born a First Lady or a Senator. During the summer, I recorded an interview for TG4 and one of the questions I was asked sparked a trail of thought that forced me to view my life from the outside, looking in. A friend of my father's would counter any perceived crises in his working life by saying: 'we are only passing through.' It was my birthday but the white-water rafting was shut. A few months before starting to write this book, I celebrated my sixtieth birthday. They take you back, those hymns, those chanted psalms, those supremely confident words sung to graceful music. I am Patrick, a sinner, the most unlearned of men, the lowliest of all the faithful, utterly worthless in the eyes of many. I was born on March 2nd, 1921, into an observant, Jewish, middle-class family in Bratislava, then part of Czechoslovakia. It's in there all the time, looking for a way out. I was always determined to make my mark in this wonderful yet often so weird game of football. I was lying in my sleeping bag, staring at the light filtering through the red and green fabric of the dome tent. The Gaelic Athletic Association had no presence on the island where I grew up. Lou Levy, top man of Leeds Music Publishing company, took me up in a taxi to the Pythian Temple on West 70th Street to show me the pocket sized recording studio where Bill Haley and His Comets had recorded "Rock Around the Clock" — then down to Jack Dempsey's restaurant on 58th and Broadway, where we sat down in a red leather upholstered booth facing the front window. This is the year that I'm going to become horticulturally correct. The year began with lunch. The first thing I remember is the gramophone arriving. I fled Tibet on 31 March 1959. The morning of May 10, 1940, was fine all over Europe. My love for Northern Ireland and the people who inhabit our community has been the underlying theme of my whole life. When the idea first came up that I should let my name stand for

TRAVEL

In his diary, written originally for RTÉ Radio, Paul Durcan remembers a chastening lesson concerning the unimportance of being Irish.

On the corner of West Ninetieth and Columbus I stand with my overweight suitcase and my forty carrier bags. Within less than a minute a Yellow Cab pulls in.

The driver is about the same age as myself, just a little younger, tall, lean, black as his leather jacket with a blue sheen from his skin that matches his blue jeans.

'Where you from?' he croons.

'Ireland.'

'Island?'

'No, Ireland.'

'Where is Island?'

'It's in the sea near England.'

'Of course it's in the sea, man. Island isn't it?'

'No, IRE-Land.'

'I don't know it, I just don't know it, man.'

Silence while I wrestle with my humiliation. With zest and humour the driver has put me in my place or, rather, not in my place.

– Paul Durcan, *Paul Durcan's Diary*

Looking through your photo
album, do you remember . . .

THE WORST TRIP EVER?

GOING ABROAD?

A RENTED HOLIDAY COTTAGE?

GOING CAMPING?

VISITING A FAMILY MEMBER
IN ANOTHER COUNTRY?

YOUR FIRST TRAIN JOURNEY?

YOUR FIRST FLIGHT?

TAKING THE MAIL BOAT?

GOING ON SAFARI?

WORKING IN A KIBBUTZ?

STUDYING YOGA IN INDIA?

GOING ON A PILGRIMAGE?

HITCH-HIKING?

TRYING TO SQUEEZE INTO LAST
YEAR'S SWIMMING TOGS?

KEEPING A TRAVEL DIARY?

GETTING SUNBURNT?

ARRIVING IN THE MIDDLE OF A FIESTA?

TREKKING THROUGH HILLS?

FIRST LINES

I remember the strange humidity during that first September in the city.

FROM *Homage to Barcelona*
BY COLM TÓIBÍN
FIRST PUBLISHED BY
SIMON & SCHUSTER
LONDON, 2000

FIRST LINES

On my tenth birthday
a bicycle and an atlas
coincided as presents and
a few days later I decided
to cycle to India.

FROM *Full Tilt*
BY DERVLA MURPHY
FIRST PUBLISHED BY
JOHN MURRAY (PUBLISHERS)
LONDON, 1965

FIRST LINES

One month after I had
started my journey
around the circumference
of America, I was back
again where I began,
on the frantic concourse
at Penn Station, in
Madison Square Gardens,
New York –
I hate neat endings.

FROM *Stranger On A Train*
BY JENNY DISKI
FIRST PUBLISHED BY
VIRAGO PRESS
LONDON, 2002

FIRST LINES

They say flying can do strange things to your mind, and an aeroplane is not the best place to commit thoughts to paper, but what the hell: this little diary of a year in the life of a professional rugby player has to start somewhere, and cruising at 550 mph at 37,000 feet with my feet up seems as good a place as any.

FROM *A Year in the Centre*
BY BRIAN O'DRISCOLL
FIRST PUBLISHED BY
PENGUIN IRELAND
DUBLIN, 2005

president of Czechoslovakia, it seemed like an absurd joke. At four o' clock in the afternoon of Thursday 24 October 1963, I was in Rome, in my room at the Hotel Minerva; I was to fly home the next day and I was putting papers away when the telephone rang. In the mid-1950s, when I was fourteen or fifteen, I told my mother I was homosexual: that was the word, back then, *homosexual*, in its full satanic majesty, cloaked in ether fumes, a combination of evil and sickness. Caron and I never talked about death – only about life. A few months after the accident I had an idea for a short film about a quadriplegic who lives in a dream. Long, long before I came to know and love Africa as a place, I yearned for it as an idea. In the fall of 1995, after resigning from my last academic post, I decided to indulge myself and fulfill a dream. I tried to hide the secrets of my past from my wife for as long as I could. Deir siad go bhfuil an fhírinne searbh, ach, creid mise ní searbh atá sí ach garbh, agus sin an fáth a seachantar í. I hope I will be able to confide everything to you, as I have never been able to confide in anyone, and I hope you will be a great source of comfort and support. On the floor in a corner of my study, sticking out from under a pile of other papers, is a shabby old green folder containing a manuscript I believe will tell me a lot about my family and my own past. It is always difficult to find a beginning. It is with a kind of fear that I begin to write the history of my life. I am consumed by memories and they form the life of me; stories that make up my life and lend it whatever veracity and purpose it may have. Here is a memory. My mother didn't try to stab my father until I was six, but she must have shown signs of oddness before that. My father and mother should have stayed in New York where they met and married and where I was born. I knew very little about my antecedents until I began writing this book. At the age of fifteen my grandmother became the concubine of a warlord general, the police chief of a tenuous national government of China. On 4 May 1923 I was born, but in giving me life my mother sacrificed her own.

EDUCATION

IN HIS MEMOIR, *The Time of My Life*, GAY BYRNE REMEMBERS HIS SCHOOLDAYS IN SYNGE STREET.

The real world hit me in the shape of Synge Street Christian Brothers' school. It was housed in a series of tall old tenement houses that had been knocked together, and the boys were divided by year into A and B streams, the groups being divided merely by a notional partition. I was always in the B stream: but the Bs in Synger were of a pretty high standard. My examination results would have been typical. I got five honours in the Inter and seven in the Leaving. The As would have got, respectively, seven and nine.

The buildings were totally unsuitable for school use. There was even an ordinary family resident in the basement, from whose radio the strains of 'Housewives' Choice' wafted upwards throughout the upper floors. On a rainy day the stench from the wet coats heaped on the jumble of bicycles on the stairways and in the halls was overpowering, as forty or more of us scrunched up together on top of each other and the unfortunate teachers in rooms designed for single families. The A class would be in the living-room of one old house and the B in the adjoining dining-room. The din was frightful: there was no getting away from what the other class was doing. While the other class was doing maths, we could hear every word – and every beating – while we were trying to concentrate on Irish, and vice versa.

– Gay Byrne, *The Time of My Life*

Cast your mind back.
Do you recall . . .

your first day at school?

who you sat next to?

your first teacher?

your teachers' nicknames?

your classmates?

the school bully?

your favourite subject?

your worst subject?

getting punished?

being suspended or even
expelled?

school lunches?

cramming for exams?

any extra-curricular activities?

any defining moments?

studying at third level?

staying awake during night
classes?

graduation day?

The school was new, like everything around us.

FROM *In My Father's House*
BY SEÁN DUNNE
FIRST PUBLISHED BY
THE GALLERY PRESS
OLDCASTLE, CO. MEATH, 2000

FIRST LINES

There is no doubt but
youth is a fine thing
though my own is not
over yet and wisdom
comes with age.

FROM *Twenty Years A-Growing*
BY MAURICE O'SULLIVAN
FIRST PUBLISHED BY
CHATTO & WINDUS
LONDON, 1933

FIRST LINES

'All advice is perfectly useless,' my father told me when he sent me away to school.

FROM *Where There's a Will*
BY JOHN MORTIMER
FIRST PUBLISHED BY
VIKING
LONDON, 2003

FIRST LINES

At the time of my father's execution and of the 1916 Rising, I was at school in Paris.

FROM *That Day's Struggle,*
A Memoir 1904-1951
BY SEÁN MACBRIDE
(EDITED BY CAITRIONA LAWLOR)
FIRST PUBLISHED BY
CURRACH PRESS
DUBLIN, 2005

I got my first lessons from my parents and, like most children, I learned the basic rules of survival and life-skills before my school years in Rush began at the age of five. Early on the morning of August 19, 1946, I was born under a clear sky after a violent summer storm to a widowed mother in the Julia Chester Hospital in Hope, a town of about six thousand in south-west Arkansas, thirty-three miles east of the Texas border at Texarkana. I sat cross-legged on the floor of the tiny home I'd created out of cardboard boxes. When you're small you know nothing. However long we may live, we never forget the time when we were young. It started with the stuff of memory, which for me meant the four most enduring memories of my teen years. My Mother was appalled at what I proposed to do – and not for the first time. At the age of twenty I was released from an internment camp without money or job. I cannot remember when these curious moments of suspense first began, when I would find myself unanchored and adrift in the dark, groping for clues as to where I was. When I was about eight, or maybe nine, my friend Ron introduced me to a life of crime. When you're a child, and you're poor, and you live next to other people who are poor, you never think of yourself as being poor. Bono sidles up to me and gives me a great, big smile. One of my earliest memories is of a little boy hanging out of the second-floor window of a house overlooking the Square in Mountmellick, County Laois. Frank Lahiffe loved Mary O'Dwyer as well. Dylan told me that he loved me the very first night we met, and although I had made love before, this was something that no other man had ever said to me. Mike and I were childhood sweethearts. Most of my adult life has been spent loving one man. In the summer of 1967, when I was ten years old, my father caved in to my persistent pleas and took me to get my own dog. A slight sound woke me, and when I opened my eyes, I was staring into the face of a lion. Ní rabhas mórán thar dhá bhliain go leith i Londain Shasana an tráth úd, ach mar sin féin, ní mórán achair eile a d'fhanfainn ann dá mbeadh –

WORK

NELL McCAFFERTY, IN HER AUTO-
BIOGRAPHY Nell, REMEMBERS HER
EARLY DAYS AS A JOURNALIST IN
The Irish Times AT THE BEGINNING
OF AN ERA.

The man who met me in the newsroom was not Donal Foley, but his deputy. The balding, mild-mannered wee man clearly did not know what to do with me. So he brought me across to what he called the 'Women's Page' desk. There were no women there. He told me to read this 'Women's Page' and get an idea of what I would be doing. It was devoted to cookery, fashion and babies. I knew nothing of these things and had no interest in them. I sat there, miserably, pretending to read. Eventually, Donal Foley arrived in, late. He came over with a wide smile and said he had read about the court case. 'You're a journalist now. You'll have to give up that kind of thing,' he said. I was panicking inside. He had hired me precisely because I came from the Bogside, and now I was being told not to act like a Bogsider any more. I sat there, doing nothing, and the clattering of typewriters, by dozens of people, the majority of them men, made things worse – how could anybody concentrate with that level of noise?

Gradually, Maeve Binchy, Mary Maher and Mary Cummins took their places at the women's desk. The four of us went to lunch with Donal, in the nearby Harp Bar and Restaurant. It was a liquid lunch, my first ever. I took to it like a duck to water, and went back to the office half-cut. This was great, but it could hardly be called work.

– Nell McCafferty, Nell

WHAT RECOLLECTIONS DO YOU
HAVE OF . . .

THE FIRST TIME YOU GOT PAID?

A PART-TIME JOB YOU DID WHILE
STILL AT SCHOOL OR COLLEGE?

YOUR FIRST REAL JOB?

SENDING MONEY HOME?

THE DIFFERENT JOBS YOU'VE HAD?

WHAT YOU LEARNED ABOUT YOURSELF
IN YOUR EARLY WORKING LIFE?

WHAT YOUR EARLY CAREER
CHOICES WERE?

WHICH JOB YOU WERE BEST AT?

WHICH JOB YOU ENJOYED MOST?

YOUR FIRST BOSS?

YOUR WORST BOSS?

THE PERSON WHO MOST INSPIRED
YOU AT WORK?

YOUR ASPIRATIONS – HAVE THEY
CHANGED OVER THE YEARS?

In Alsace, round about 1850, a schoolmaster, burdened with children, agreed to become a grocer.

FROM *Words*
BY JEAN-PAUL SARTRE
FIRST PUBLISHED BY
EDITIONS GALLIMARD
PARIS, 1964

FIRST LINES

I wasn't born a First Lady
or a Senator.

FROM *Living History*
BY HILLARY RODHAM CLINTON
FIRST PUBLISHED BY
SIMON & SCHUSTER
NEW YORK, 2003

FIRST LINES

During the summer, I recorded an interview for TG4 and one of the questions I was asked sparked a trail of thought that forced me to view my life from the outside, looking in.

FROM *Paper Tigers*
BY MARY KENNEDY
FIRST PUBLISHED BY
MERLIN PUBLISHING
DUBLIN, 2003

FIRST LINES

A friend of my father's
would counter any
perceived crises in
his working life by saying:
'we are only passing
through.'

FROM *Passing Through*
BY DECLAN HASSETT
FIRST PUBLISHED BY
MERCIER PRESS
CORK, 2004

sea, caithfear a rá – dá mbeadh an oiread agam is a bhéarfadh abhaile mé. **The soil in Leitrim is poor, in places no more than an inch deep.** How to sort out one's confused love-hate relationship with the place that gave one birth? **I remember the strange humidity during that first September in the city.** On my tenth birthday, a bicycle and an atlas coincided as presents and a few days later I decided to cycle to India. **One month after I had started my journey around the circumference of America, I was back again where I began, on the frantic concourse at Penn Station, in Madison Square Gardens, New York — I hate neat endings.** They say flying can do strange things to your mind, and an aeroplane is not the best place to commit thoughts to paper, but what the hell: this little diary of a year in the life of a professional rugby player has to start somewhere, and cruising at 550 mph at 37,000 feet with my feet up seems as good a place as any. **The school was new, like everything around us.** There is no doubt but youth is a fine thing though my own is not over yet and wisdom comes with age. **'All advice is perfectly useless,' my father told me when he sent me away to school.** At the time of my father's execution and of the 1916 Rising, I was at school in Paris. **In Alsace, round about 1850, a schoolmaster, burdened with children, agreed to become a grocer.** I wasn't born a First Lady or a Senator. **During the summer, I recorded an interview for TG4 and one of the questions I was asked sparked a trail of thought that forced me to view my life from the outside, looking in.** A friend of my father's would counter any perceived crises in his working life by saying: 'we are only passing through.' **It was my birthday but the white-water rafting was shut.** A few months before starting to write this book, I celebrated my sixtieth birthday. **They take you back, those hymns, those chanted psalms, those supremely confident words sung to graceful music.** I am Patrick, a sinner, the most unlearned of men, the lowliest of all the faithful, utterly worthless in the eyes of many. **I was born on March 2nd, 1921, into an observant, Jewish, middle-class family in**

CELEBRATIONS

IN AN EXTRACT FROM *Misadventures in Motherhood*, FIONA LOONEY RECALLS TWO REASONS FOR DISLIKING THE ST PATRICK'S DAY PARADE.

The St Patrick's Day Parade killed my great-grandfather and I have had an ambivalent attitude towards it ever since. It never came to court, of course – and if it had, it's likely that the defence would have argued that it was less the parade itself than my great-grandfather's attending it without his overcoat that led to the pneumonia that ensured he never marked his fiftieth birthday. But legal argument cuts no dice with a four-year-old, so when I was heading out for my very first parade – and my grandmother cautioned me to wrap up well because her father had died as a direct result of being negligent in the overcoat department on just such a day as this – well, let's just say that all the baton twirling in the cosmos couldn't have salvaged that parade or any of the excruciating ones that followed it.

Aside from its decimation of my family, I had a second issue with the St Patrick's Day Parade. As a person of unimpressive stature – both then and now – I grew tired of staring at the back of strangers' (over)coats for two hours at a time, knowing that other people were having a grand old time just feet away from me.

– Fiona Looney, *Misadventures in Motherhood*

WHAT CAN YOU WRITE ABOUT . . .

THE BEST BIRTHDAY PARTY
YOU EVER HAD?

TURNING 30, AND THEN 40,
AND THEN 50 . . . ?

THE MOST GLAMOROUS OUTFIT YOU
BOUGHT FOR A CELEBRATION?

THE BEST FANCY DRESS YOU EVER
WENT TO?

THE ODDEST EVENT YOU EVER
ATTENDED?

YOUR MOST ROMANTIC
ST VALENTINE'S DAY?

YOUR WEDDING DAY?

THE BEST SURPRISE YOU EVER
ORGANISED FOR SOMEONE?

THE MOST TIRING CHILDREN'S PARTY
YOU EVER HOSTED?

YOUR FAVOURITE PRESENT?

THE GIFT YOU BROUGHT STRAIGHT
BACK TO THE SHOP?

BECOMING A PARENT FOR
THE FIRST TIME?

THE BEST PARADE YOU EVER SAW?

FIRST LINES

It was my birthday but the white-water rafting was shut.

FROM *Rogue Trader*
BY NICK LEESON
FIRST PUBLISHED BY
LITTLE, BROWN AND CO.
LONDON, 1996

FIRST LINES

A few months before starting to write this book, I celebrated my sixtieth birthday.

3

FROM *Not Quite the Diplomat*
BY CHRIS PATTEN
FIRST PUBLISHED BY
ALLEN LANE
LONDON, 2005

Bratislava, then part of Czechoslovakia. It's in there all the time, looking for a way out. I was always determined to make my mark in this wonderful yet often so weird game of football. I was lying in my sleeping bag, staring at the light filtering through the red and green fabric of the dome tent. The Gaelic Athletic Association had no presence on the island where I grew up. Lou Levy, top man of Leeds Music Publishing company, took me up in a taxi to the Pythian Temple on West 70th Street to show me the pocket sized recording studio where Bill Haley and His Comets had recorded "Rock Around the Clock" — then down to Jack Dempsey's restaurant on 58th and Broadway, where we sat down in a red leather upholstered booth facing the front window. This is the year that I'm going to become horticulturally correct. The year began with lunch. The first thing I remember is the gramophone arriving. I fled Tibet on 31 March 1959. The morning of May 10, 1940, was fine all over Europe. My love for Northern Ireland and the people who inhabit our community has been the underlying theme of my whole life. When the idea first came up that I should let my name stand for president of Czechoslovakia, it seemed like an absurd joke. At four o' clock in the afternoon of Thursday 24 October 1963, I was in Rome, in my room at the Hotel Minerva; I was to fly home the next day and I was putting papers away when the telephone rang. In the mid-1950s, when I was fourteen or fifteen, I told my mother I was homosexual: that was the word, back then, *homosexual*, in its full satanic majesty, cloaked in ether fumes, a combination of evil and sickness. Caron and I never talked about death — only about life. A few months after the accident I had an idea for a short film about a quadriplegic who lives in a dream. Long, long before I came to know and love Africa as a place, I yearned for it as an idea. In the fall of 1995, after resigning from my last academic post, I decided to indulge myself and fulfill a dream. I tried to hide the secrets of my past from my wife for as long as I could. Deir siad go bhfuil an fhírinne searbh, ach, creid mise ní searbh atá sí

FAITH

IN THIS PASSAGE FROM *The Sign of the Cross*, COLM TÓIBÍN REMEMBERS THE RETURNING PILGRIMS OF HIS CHILDHOOD, HIS FIRST INTIMATIONS OF A WORLD OUTSIDE IRELAND.

My mother and my aunt had just been sleeping; they were tired. They had travelled overland to Lourdes.

'Overland': that was one of the new words that suddenly became commonplace as the story of the journey was told. 'Basilica', 'Courier', 'Down through France'. There was no fizzy orange to be had in France, and the heat was terrible in the bus, and everybody was dying of thirst. A bottle of orange juice cost a lot of money, but still it was worth it. It was so hot in France.

Postcards came of torchlit processions, or of Saint Bernadette, or of the statue of Our Lady of Lourdes. There were large plastic bottles of Lourdes water with shoulder straps, or smaller bottles in the shape of Our Lady of Lourdes with a blue screw-cap top. These were my first intimations of the world outside Ireland. My parents and aunts and uncles went to Lourdes, sometimes venturing over the border to San Sebastian in Spain. One aunt, my father's sister, went on pilgrimages to Rome and Santiago de Compostela. All along the mantelpiece of the back room at home there were souvenirs from these journeys – an ashtray of Toledo gold, a small, ornamental sword in a leather scabbard, a holy statue.

– Colm Tóibín, *The Sign of the Cross*

CAN YOU REMEMBER. . .

WHAT YOU THOUGHT ABOUT
RELIGION AS A CHILD?

A FAVOURITE HYMN OR PRAYER?

A SAINT OR PROPHET YOU LIKED?

EVER WANTING TO BE A PRIEST,
A MONK OR A NUN?

HOW IMPORTANT RELIGION WAS
TO YOUR FAMILY?

BEING BORED IN CHURCH?

EVER WANTING TO STUDY BUDDHISM?

ATTENDING SUNDAY SCHOOL?

OBSERVING THE SABBATH?

YOUR FIRST HOLY COMMUNION
SUIT OR DRESS?

BEING AN ALTAR BOY OR GIRL?

HOW YOUR BELIEFS HAVE CHANGED
OVER THE YEARS?

A HEALING PILGRIMAGE?

THE POPE COMING TO IRELAND?

FIRST LINES

They take you back, those hymns, those chanted psalms, those supremely confident words sung to graceful music.

FROM *Another Country*
BY GENE KERRIGAN
FIRST PUBLISHED BY
GILL & MACMILLAN
DUBLIN, 1998

I am Patrick, a sinner, the
most unlearned of men,
the lowliest of all the
faithful, utterly worthless
in the eyes of many.

FROM *Confessio*
BY SAINT PATRICK
AS PUBLISHED IN
Patrick in His Own Words
BY JOSEPH DUFFY
VERITAS PUBLICATIONS
DUBLIN, 1972

FIRST LINES

I was born on March 2nd, 1921, into an observant, Jewish, middle-class family in Bratislava, then part of Czechoslovakia.

FROM *My Stamp On Life*
BY MAX STERN
FIRST PUBLISHED BY
MAKOR JEWISH
COMMUNITY LIBRARY
VICTORIA, AUSTRALIA, 2003

ach garbh, agus sin an fáth a seachantar í. I hope I will be able to confide everything to you, as I have never been able to confide in anyone, and I hope you will be a great source of comfort and support. On the floor in a corner of my study, sticking out from under a pile of other papers, is a shabby old green folder containing a manuscript I believe will tell me a lot about my family and my own past. It is always difficult to find a beginning. It is with a kind of fear that I begin to write the history of my life. I am consumed by memories and they form the life of me; stories that make up my life and lend it whatever veracity and purpose it may have. Here is a memory. My mother didn't try to stab my father until I was six, but she must have shown signs of oddness before that. My father and mother should have stayed in New York where they met and married and where I was born. I knew very little about my antecedents until I began writing this book. At the age of fifteen my grandmother became the concubine of a warlord general, the police chief of a tenuous national government of China. On 4 May 1923 I was born, but in giving me life my mother sacrificed her own. I got my first lessons from my parents and, like most children, I learned the basic rules of survival and life-skills before my school years in Rush began at the age of five. Early on the morning of August 19, 1946, I was born under a clear sky after a violent summer storm to a widowed mother in the Julia Chester Hospital in Hope, a town of about six thousand in south-west Arkansas, thirty-three miles east of the Texas border at Texarkana. I sat cross-legged on the floor of the tiny home I'd created out of cardboard boxes. When you're small you know nothing. However long we may live, we never forget the time when we were young. It started with the stuff of memory, which for me meant the four most enduring memories of my teen years. My Mother was appalled at what I proposed to do – and not for the first time. At the age of twenty I was released from an internment camp without money or job. I cannot remember when these curious moments of suspense first

SPORT

IN *From Dún Síon to Croke Park*
MICHEÁL Ó MUIRCHEARTAIGH
DESCRIBES HIS FIRST VISIT TO
CROKE PARK.

One of the great advantages of Pat's was its proximity to Croke Park, hardly a mile away. I had not long to wait for my first visit. There was neither talk nor a need of a ticket as a few of us set off to see the All-Ireland football final between Cavan and Mayo.

It was a much different Croke Park then, with standing the order of the day for more than 80 per cent of spectators. On the east side of the pitch, the tall Cusack Stand, supported by huge pillars, seated about 6,000 spectators, with standing room underneath. There were three stands on the opposite side. The Long Stand, a plain structure with a low corrugated-iron roof that gave protection from the elements, ranged from the corner flag at the Canal End to roughly midfield. It was more a barn with an opening on one side than a stand, and it was common for spectators to climb on to the roof for comfort on big days. On the other side of the broadcasting box, the Hogan Stand ran towards the Railway End; it was the fashionable area. Beyond the Hogan was the Corner Stand. We found ourselves standing under the Cusack close enough to Hill 16, the famous terrace at the Railway End – an ideal position as events unfolded.

– Micheál Ó Muircheartaigh, *From Dún Síon to Croke Park*

WHAT WOULD YOU LIKE TO
RECORD ABOUT....

YOUR FAVOURITE SPORT?

THE SPORTS YOU PLAYED?

YOUR GREATEST SPORTING MOMENT?

YOUR TEAM'S GREATEST TRIUMPH?

YOUR FIRST MEDAL?

AN INJURY THAT REALLY HURT?

A DEFEAT THAT HURT EVEN MORE?

THE ATHLETE YOU ADMIRED MOST?

YOUR TOUGHEST OPPONENT?

THE BEST EVENT YOU EVER WATCHED?

THE MOST IMPRESSIVE STADIUM YOU
EVER VISITED?

THE FURTHEST YOU TRAVELLED
TO WATCH AN EVENT?

BEING AN ARMCHAIR ATHLETE?

FIRST LINES

It's in there all the time,
looking for a way out.

FROM *Fever Pitch*
BY NICK HORNBY
FIRST PUBLISHED BY
VICTOR GOLLANCZ
LONDON, 1992

FIRST LINES

I was always determined to make my mark in this wonderful yet often so weird game of football.

FROM *Hard Tackles and Dirty Baths*
BY GEORGE BEST
FIRST PUBLISHED BY
EBURY PRESS
LONDON, 2005

FIRST LINES

I was lying in my sleeping bag, staring at the light filtering through the red and green fabric of the dome tent.

FROM *Touching the Void*
BY JOE SIMPSON
FIRST PUBLISHED BY
JONATHAN CAPE
LONDON, 1988

FIRST LINES

The Gaelic Athletic Association had no presence on the island where I grew up.

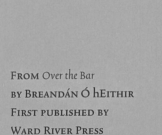

FROM *Over the Bar*
BY BREANDÁN Ó hEITHIR
FIRST PUBLISHED BY
WARD RIVER PRESS
DUBLIN, 1984

began, when I would find myself unanchored and adrift in the dark, groping for clues as to where I was. When I was about eight, or maybe nine, my friend Ron introduced me to a life of crime. When you're a child, and you're poor, and you live next to other people who are poor, you never think of yourself as being poor. Bono sidles up to me and gives me a great, big smile. One of my earliest memories is of a little boy hanging out of the second-floor window of a house overlooking the Square in Mountmellick, County Laois. Frank Lahiffe loved Mary O'Dwyer as well. Dylan told me that he loved me the very first night we met, and although I had made love before, this was something that no other man had ever said to me. Mike and I were childhood sweethearts. Most of my adult life has been spent loving one man. In the summer of 1967, when I was ten years old, my father caved in to my persistent pleas and took me to get my own dog. A slight sound woke me, and when I opened my eyes, I was staring into the face of a lion. Ní rabhas mórán thar dhá bhliain go leith i Londain Shasana an tráth úd, ach mar sin féin, ní mórán achair eile a d'fhanfainn ann dá mbeadh — sea, caithfear a rá — dá mbeadh an oiread agam is a bhéarfadh abhaile mé. The soil in Leitrim is poor, in places no more than an inch deep. How to sort out one's confused love-hate relationship with the place that gave one birth? I remember the strange humidity during that first September in the city. On my tenth birthday, a bicycle and an atlas coincided as presents and a few days later I decided to cycle to India. One month after I had started my journey around the circumference of America, I was back again where I began, on the frantic concourse at Penn Station, in Madison Square Gardens, New York — I hate neat endings. They say flying can do strange things to your mind, and an aeroplane is not the best place to commit thoughts to paper, but what the hell: this little diary of a year in the life of a professional rugby player has to start somewhere, and cruising at 550 mph at 37,000 feet with my feet up seems as good a place as any. The school was new, like

PASTIMES

IN THIS PASSAGE FROM HIS MEMOIR, CHRISTY BROWN REMEMBERS THE JOY OF DISCOVERING THAT HE WAS ABLE TO PAINT WITH HIS LEFT FOOT.

I was changing. I didn't know it then, but I had found a way to be happy again and to forget some of the things that had made me unhappy. Above all I learned to forget myself. I didn't miss going out with my brothers now, for I had something to keep my mind active, something to make each day, a thing to look forward to.

I would sit crouched on the floor for hours, holding the brush between my toes, my right leg curled up under my left, my arms held tightly at my sides, the hands clenched. All my paints and brushes were around me, and I would get mother or father to pin the drawing paper to the floor with tacks to keep it steady. It looked a very queer awkward position, with my head almost between my knees and my back as crooked as a corkscrew. But I painted all my best pictures in this way, with the wooden floor as my only easel.

– Christy Brown, *My Left Foot*

WHAT DO YOU REMEMBER ABOUT . . .

YOUR FAVOURITE PASTIMES
AS A CHILD?

HOBBIES YOU HAD OVER THE YEARS?

THE MUSIC YOU LOVED TO LISTEN TO?

FILMS YOU LOVED TO WATCH?

COMICS YOU READ?

WRITERS WHO INFLUENCED YOU?

PROGRAMMES THAT HELD YOU
SPELLBOUND?

COOKING A GOURMET MEAL?

THINGS YOU COLLECTED?

PLANTING YOUR FIRST GARDEN?

PAINTING?

CRAFT CLASSES?

PEOPLE WHO GOT YOU INTERESTED
IN THINGS?

A TEACHER WHO MADE A DIFFERENCE?

THE FIRST JUMPER YOU EVER KNITTED?

COMPETITIONS YOU WON OR LOST?

AWARDS YOU RECEIVED?

FIRST LINES

Lou Levy, top man of Leeds Music Publishing company, took me up in a taxi to the Pythian Temple on West 70th Street to show me the pocket sized recording studio where Bill Haley and His Comets had recorded "Rock Around the Clock" – then down to Jack Dempsey's restaurant on 58th and Broadway, where we sat down in a red leather upholstered booth facing the front window.

FROM *Chronicles*
BY BOB DYLAN
FIRST PUBLISHED BY
SIMON & SCHUSTER UK
LONDON, 2004

FIRST LINES

This is the year that I'm going to become horticulturally correct.

FROM *Helen Dillon On Gardening*
BY HELEN DILLON
FIRST PUBLISHED BY
TOWNHOUSE
DUBLIN, 1998

FIRST LINES

The year began with lunch.

FROM *A Year In Provence*
BY PETER MAYLE
FIRST PUBLISHED BY
HAMISH HAMILTON
LONDON, 1989

The first thing I remember is the gramophone arriving.

FROM *Rory & Ita*
BY RODDY DOYLE
JONATHAN CAPE
LONDON, 2002

everything around us. There is no doubt but youth is a fine thing though my own is not over yet and wisdom comes with age. 'All advice is perfectly useless,' my father told me when he sent me away to school. At the time of my father's execution and of the 1916 Rising, I was at school in Paris. In Alsace, round about 1850, a schoolmaster, burdened with children, agreed to become a grocer. I wasn't born a First Lady or a Senator. During the summer, I recorded an interview for TG4 and one of the questions I was asked sparked a trail of thought that forced me to view my life from the outside, looking in. A friend of my father's would counter any perceived crises in his working life by saying: 'we are only passing through.' It was my birthday but the white-water rafting was shut. A few months before starting to write this book, I celebrated my sixtieth birthday. They take you back, those hymns, those chanted psalms, those supremely confident words sung to graceful music. I am Patrick, a sinner, the most unlearned of men, the lowliest of all the faithful, utterly worthless in the eyes of many. I was born on March 2nd, 1921, into an observant, Jewish, middle-class family in Bratislava, then part of Czechoslovakia. It's in there all the time, looking for a way out. I was always determined to make my mark in this wonderful yet often so weird game of football. I was lying in my sleeping bag, staring at the light filtering through the red and green fabric of the dome tent. The Gaelic Athletic Association had no presence on the island where I grew up. Lou Levy, top man of Leeds Music Publishing company, took me up in a taxi to the Pythian Temple on West 70th Street to show me the pocket sized recording studio where Bill Haley and His Comets had recorded "Rock Around the Clock" — then down to Jack Dempsey's restaurant on 58th and Broadway, where we sat down in a red leather upholstered booth facing the front window. This is the year that I'm going to become horticulturally correct. The year began with lunch. The first thing I remember is the gramophone arriving. I fled Tibet on 31 March 1959. The morning of May 10, 1940, was fine all over

CITIZENSHIP

Then he started making speeches. Not everybody had a radio and not everybody could read the newspapers at that time, so they went to hear people making speeches on O'Connell Street instead. The way you knew that people agreed with what you were saying is that they suddenly threw their hats and caps up in the air and cheered. The biggest crowd with the most amount of hats going up was always outside the GPO for de Valera. Some people had loudspeakers, but the good speakers needed nothing, only their own voices, and my uncle Ted says the best of them all was further up the street, a man named James Larkin who had a great way of stretching his arms out over the crowd.

My father wouldn't throw his hat up for anyone, so he started making his own speeches at the other end of the street with his friends. They had their own newspaper and their own leaflets and a party pin in the shape of a small 'e' for Éire: Ireland. He said it was time for Ireland to stand up on its own two feet and become a real country, not a place you dreamed about.

– Hugo Hamilton, *The Speckled People*

CAN YOU REMEMBER. . .

ORGANISING A LOCAL CAMPAIGN?

FUNDRAISING FOR A GOOD CAUSE?

SETTING UP A CLUB?

THE FIRST TIME YOU VOTED?

WORKING TO IMPROVE YOUR
ENVIRONMENT?

VOLUNTEERING AT HOME
OR ELSEWHERE?

ATTENDING A PEACE MARCH?

FEELING RESPONSIBLE, HOPELESS,
OR OUTRAGED?

THE LOCAL LEADER WHO GOT
THINGS DONE?

THE ISSUES FACING YOUR COMMUNITY?

YOUR FAMILY'S POLITICAL ALLEGIANCES?

YOUR VIEWS ON POLITICIANS?

CANVASSING AT ELECTION TIME?

STANDING FOR OFFICE?

BEING INVOLVED IN DEBATES?

ELECTIONS WON AND LOST?

FIRST LINES

I fled Tibet

on 31 March 1959.

FROM *Freedom In Exile*
BY THE DALAI LAMA
FIRST PUBLISHED BY
HODDER AND STOUGHTON
LONDON, 1990

The morning of
May 10, 1940, was fine
all over Europe.

FROM *Memoirs*
BY JEAN MONNET
FIRST PUBLISHED BY
DOUBLEDAY & COMPANY
NEW YORK, 1978

FIRST LINES

My love for Northern Ireland and the people who inhabit our community has been the underlying theme of my whole life.

FROM *Willie John – The Story of My Life*
BY WILLIE JOHN MCBRIDE
FIRST PUBLISHED BY
PORTRAIT
LONDON, 2004

FIRST LINES

When the idea first came up that I should let my name stand for president of Czechoslovakia, it seemed like an absurd joke.

FROM *Summer Meditations*
BY VÁCLAV HAVEL
FIRST PUBLISHED BY
FABER AND FABER
LONDON, 1992

Europe. My love for Northern Ireland and the people who inhabit our community has been the underlying theme of my whole life. When the idea first came up that I should let my name stand for president of Czechoslovakia, it seemed like an absurd joke. At four o' clock in the afternoon of Thursday 24 October 1963, I was in Rome, in my room at the Hotel Minerva; I was to fly home the next day and I was putting papers away when the telephone rang. In the mid-1950s, when I was fourteen or fifteen, I told my mother I was homosexual: that was the word, back then, *homosexual*, in its full satanic majesty, cloaked in ether fumes, a combination of evil and sickness. Caron and I never talked about death – only about life. A few months after the accident I had an idea for a short film about a quadriplegic who lives in a dream. Long, long before I came to know and love Africa as a place, I yearned for it as an idea. In the fall of 1995, after resigning from my last academic post, I decided to indulge myself and fulfill a dream. I tried to hide the secrets of my past from my wife for as long as I could. Deir siad go bhfuil an fhírinne searbh, ach, creid mise ní searbh atá sí ach garbh, agus sin an fáth a seachantar í. I hope I will be able to confide everything to you, as I have never been able to confide in anyone, and I hope you will be a great source of comfort and support. On the floor in a corner of my study, sticking out from under a pile of other papers, is a shabby old green folder containing a manuscript I believe will tell me a lot about my family and my own past. It is always difficult to find a beginning. It is with a kind of fear that I begin to write the history of my life. I am consumed by memories and they form the life of me; stories that make up my life and lend it whatever veracity and purpose it may have. Here is a memory. My mother didn't try to stab my father until I was six, but she must have shown signs of oddness before that. My father and mother should have stayed in New York where they met and married and where I was born. I knew very little about my antecedents until I began writing this book. At the age of fifteen

TURNING POINTS

IN HIS MEMOIR, *Is That It?*, BOB GELDOF REMEMBERS THE EXACT MOMENT HIS ATTENTION WAS DRAWN TO THE PLIGHT OF AFRICA.

The camera wandered amidst them like a mesmerized observer, occasionally dwelling on one person so that he looked directly at me, sitting in my comfortable living room surrounded by the fripperies of modern living which we were pleased to regard as necessities. Their eyes looked into mine. There was an emaciated woman too weak to do anything but limply hold her dying child. There was a skeletal man holding out a bundle wrapped in sacking so that it could be counted; it looked like a tightly wrapped package of old sticks, but it was the desiccated body of his child. And there were children, their bodies fragile and vulnerable as premature babies but with the consciousness of what was happening to them gleaming dully from their eyes. All around was the murmur of death, like a hoarse whisper, or the buzzing of flies.

Right from the first few seconds it was clear that this was a tragedy which the world had somehow contrived not to notice until it had reached a scale which constituted an international scandal. You could hear that in the tones of the reporter. It was not the usual dispassionate objectivity of the BBC. It was the voice of a man who was registering despair, grief and absolute disgust at what he was seeing. At the end the newscaster remained silent. Paula burst into tears, and then rushed upstairs to check on our baby who was sleeping peacefully in her cot.

– Bob Geldof, Is That It?

CAN YOU IDENTIFY A DEFINING
MOMENT FOR YOU? WAS IT . . .

AN EVENT OR PLACE THAT CHANGED
YOUR OUTLOOK?

A PICTURE OR A PIECE OF WRITING
THAT AFFECTED YOU?

AN ILLNESS THAT MADE YOU THINK
AGAIN?

THE DEATH OF A LOVED ONE?

FINDING SOMEONE TO LOVE?

STARTING A FAMILY?

FINALLY RESIGNING FROM THAT
JOB THAT YOU HATED?

FINDING THE PERFECT JOB?

BEING SELECTED OR ELECTED?

FINDING THAT ONE THING THAT
REALLY SUITED YOU?

MEETING SOMEONE WHO BELIEVED
IN YOU?

A 'COINCIDENCE' THAT SEEMED TO
MARK A NEW BEGINNING?

FINALLY ACCEPTING YOURSELF –
JUST THE WAY YOU ARE?

At four o' clock in the afternoon of Thursday 24 October 1963, I was in Rome, in my room at the Hotel Minerva; I was to fly home the next day and I was putting papers away when the telephone rang.

FROM *A Very Easy Death*
BY SIMONE DE BEAUVOIR
FIRST PUBLISHED BY
PENGUIN BOOKS
LONDON 1969

FIRST LINES

In the mid-1950s, when
I was fourteen or fifteen,
I told my mother I was
homosexual: that was
the word, back then,
homosexual, in its full
satanic majesty, cloaked
in ether fumes, a
combination of evil
and sickness.

From *My Lives*
by Edmund white
First published by
Bloomsbury Publishing
London, 2005

FIRST LINES

Caron and I never talked about death – only about life.

FROM *Next To You*
BY GLORIA HUNNIFORD
FIRST PUBLISHED BY
MICHAEL JOSEPH
LONDON, 2005

my grandmother became the concubine of a warlord general, the police chief of a tenuous national government of China. On 4 May 1923 I was born, but in giving me life my mother sacrificed her own. I got my first lessons from my parents and, like most children, I learned the basic rules of survival and life-skills before my school years in Rush began at the age of five. Early on the morning of August 19, 1946, I was born under a clear sky after a violent summer storm to a widowed mother in the Julia Chester Hospital in Hope, a town of about six thousand in south-west Arkansas, thirty-three miles east of the Texas border at Texarkana. I sat cross-legged on the floor of the tiny home I'd created out of cardboard boxes. When you're small you know nothing. However long we may live, we never forget the time when we were young. It started with the stuff of memory, which for me meant the four most enduring memories of my teen years. My Mother was appalled at what I proposed to do – and not for the first time. At the age of twenty I was released from an internment camp without money or job. I cannot remember when these curious moments of suspense first began, when I would find myself unanchored and adrift in the dark, groping for clues as to where I was. When I was about eight, or maybe nine, my friend Ron introduced me to a life of crime. When you're a child, and you're poor, and you live next to other people who are poor, you never think of yourself as being poor. Bono sidles up to me and gives me a great, big smile. One of my earliest memories is of a little boy hanging out of the second-floor window of a house overlooking the Square in Mountmellick, County Laois. Frank Lahiffe loved Mary O'Dwyer as well. Dylan told me that he loved me the very first night we met, and although I had made love before, this was something that no other man had ever said to me. Mike and I were childhood sweethearts. Most of my adult life has been spent loving one man. In the summer of 1967, when I was ten years old, my father caved in to my persistent pleas and took me to get my own dog. A slight sound woke me, and when

DREAMS

IN THIS PASSAGE FROM *Bridge Across My Sorrows*, CHRISTINA NOBLE TELLS OF A DREAM THAT WOULD CHANGE HER LIFE.

It was during this time in my life, at a time of great misery and pain, that I had the dream about Vietnam. I don't know why I dreamed of Vietnam. Perhaps it was because the country was so much in the news at the time. In my dream, naked Vietnamese children were running down a dirt road fleeing from a napalm bombing. The ground under the children was cracked and coming apart and the children were reaching out to me. One of the girls had a look in her eyes that implored me to pick her up and protect her and take her to safety. Above the escaping children was a brilliant white light that contained the word 'Vietnam'.

At the time, I did not even know where Vietnam was. I didn't know anything about the people there. But after that dream I knew that it was my destiny to go to Vietnam and to work with children.

– Christina Noble, *Bridge Across My Sorrows*

CLOSE YOUR EYES AND TRY
TO DESCRIBE . . .

THE KIND OF DREAMS YOU HAVE
WHEN YOU SLEEP?

A RECURRING DREAM YOU'VE
HAD SINCE CHILDHOOD?

HOW A PARTICULAR DREAM
INFLUENCED YOUR ACTIONS?

A DREAM THAT CAME TRUE?

A DREAM THAT TURNED INTO
A NIGHTMARE?

THAT TIME YOU WERE CAUGHT
DAYDREAMING?

YOUR DREAM PIN-UP?

A DREAM MEAL?

THAT DREAM HOLIDAY?

YOUR DREAM HOUSE?

A FANTASY YOU HOPED WOULD
BECOME A REALITY?

FIRST LINES

A few months after the accident I had an idea for a short film about a quadriplegic who lives in a dream.

From *Still Me*
by Christopher Reeve
First published by
Century
London, 1998

FIRST LINES

Long, long before I came
to know and love Africa
as a place, I yearned for it
as an idea.

FROM *A Passage to Africa*
BY GEORGE ALAGIAH
FIRST PUBLISHED BY
LITTLE, BROWN
LONDON, 2001

FIRST LINES

In the fall of 1995, after resigning from my last academic post, I decided to indulge myself and fulfill a dream.

FROM *Reading Lolita in Tehran*
BY AZAR NAFISI
FIRST PUBLISHED BY
I. B. TAURIS
LONDON, 2003

I opened my eyes, I was staring into the face of a lion. Ní rabhas mórán thar dhá bhliain go leith i Londain Shasana an tráth úd, ach mar sin féin, ní mórán achair eile a d'fhanfainn ann dá mbeadh – sea, caithfear a rá – dá mbeadh an oiread agam is a bhéarfadh abhaile mé. The soil in Leitrim is poor, in places no more than an inch deep. How to sort out one's confused love-hate relationship with the place that gave one birth? I remember the strange humidity during that first September in the city. On my tenth birthday, a bicycle and an atlas coincided as presents and a few days later I decided to cycle to India. One month after I had started my journey around the circumference of America, I was back again where I began, on the frantic concourse at Penn Station, in Madison Square Gardens, New York — I hate neat endings. They say flying can do strange things to your mind, and an aeroplane is not the best place to commit thoughts to paper, but what the hell: this little diary of a year in the life of a professional rugby player has to start somewhere, and cruising at 550 mph at 37,000 feet with my feet up seems as good a place as any. The school was new, like everything around us. There is no doubt but youth is a fine thing though my own is not over yet and wisdom comes with age. 'All advice is perfectly useless,' my father told me when he sent me away to school. At the time of my father's execution and of the 1916 Rising, I was at school in Paris. In Alsace, round about 1850, a schoolmaster, burdened with children, agreed to become a grocer. I wasn't born a First Lady or a Senator. During the summer, I recorded an interview for TG4 and one of the questions I was asked sparked a trail of thought that forced me to view my life from the outside, looking in. A friend of my father's would counter any perceived crises in his working life by saying: 'we are only passing through.' It was my birthday but the white-water rafting was shut. A few months before starting to write this book, I celebrated my sixtieth birthday. They take you back, those hymns, those chanted psalms, those supremely confident words sung to graceful music. I am

SECRETS

IN HER SECOND MEMOIR, *Almost There,*
NUALA O'FAOLAIN REMEMBERS
A MOMENT OF DISCOVERY ABOUT
THE LOVER SHE THOUGHT SHE KNEW.

AND I HAD KNOWN, though he had never told me. Never given a clue. I'd known not from anything obvious, like the secrecy of our affair; I somehow knew he had a wife from his worn, clean underwear. And I knew he was a father from the complacent way he issued pieces of advice – advice about my car, advice about the weather. You could feel the privilege that was extended to him in his home, that had made him so lordly.

– Nuala O'Faolain, *Almost There*

Do you . . .

WANT TO TELL A SECRET?

HAVE ANYTHING TO HIDE?

KNOW SOMETHING YOU PROMISED
NOT TO TELL?

ROUND DOWN YOUR WEIGHT?

LIE ABOUT YOUR AGE?

EVER FORGET TO PAY?

THINK HOTEL TOWELS ARE YOURS
TO KEEP?

DYE YOUR HAIR?

NEVER LET THE FACTS GET IN THE WAY
OF A GOOD STORY?

EVER HAVE SINISTER THOUGHTS?

EXAGGERATE YOUR POSITION?

THINK YOU COULD EVER BE BRIBED?

HAVE ANY REGRETS?

THINK REGRET IS POINTLESS?

FIRST LINES

I tried to hide the secrets of my past from my wife for as long as I could.

FROM *A Brother's Journey*
BY RICHARD B. PELZER
FIRST PUBLISHED BY
TIME WARNER BOOKS
LONDON, 2005

Deir siad go bhfuil an
fhírinne searbh, ach, creid
mise ní searbh atá sí ach
garbh, agus sin an fáth a
seachantar í.

As Mo Bhealach Féin
le Seosamh MacGrianna
An chéad chló
Rialtas na héireann
Baile Átha Cliath, 1940

FIRST LINES

I hope I will be able to confide everything to you, as I have never been able to confide in anyone, and I hope you will be a great source of comfort and support.

FROM *The Diary of a Young Girl*
BY ANNE FRANK
PUBLISHED BY
PENGUIN BOOKS
LONDON, 1997

On the floor in a corner of my study, sticking out from under a pile of other papers, is a shabby old green folder containing a manuscript I believe will tell me a lot about my family and my own past.

FROM *My Ear At His Heart*
BY HANIF KUREISHI
FIRST PUBLISHED BY
FABER AND FABER
LONDON, 2004

Patrick, a sinner, the most unlearned of men, the lowliest of all the faithful, utterly worthless in the eyes of many. I was born on March 2nd, 1921, into an observant, Jewish, middle-class family in Bratislava, then part of Czechoslovakia. It's in there all the time, looking for a way out. I was always determined to make my mark in this wonderful yet often so weird game of football. I was lying in my sleeping bag, staring at the light filtering through the red and green fabric of the dome tent. The Gaelic Athletic Association had no presence on the island where I grew up. Lou Levy, top man of Leeds Music Publishing company, took me up in a taxi to the Pythian Temple on West 70th Street to show me the pocket sized recording studio where Bill Haley and His Comets had recorded "Rock Around the Clock" — then down to Jack Dempsey's restaurant on 58th and Broadway, where we sat down in a red leather upholstered booth facing the front window. This is the year that I'm going to become horticulturally correct. The year began with lunch. The first thing I remember is the gramophone arriving. I fled Tibet on 31 March 1959. The morning of May 10, 1940, was fine all over Europe. My love for Northern Ireland and the people who inhabit our community has been the underlying theme of my whole life. When the idea first came up that I should let my name stand for president of Czechoslovakia, it seemed like an absurd joke. At four o' clock in the afternoon of Thursday 24 October 1963, I was in Rome, in my room at the Hotel Minerva; I was to fly home the next day and I was putting papers away when the telephone rang. In the mid-1950s, when I was fourteen or fifteen, I told my mother I was homosexual: that was the word, back then, homosexual, in its full satanic majesty, cloaked in ether fumes, a combination of evil and sickness. Caron and I never talked about death – only about life. A few months after the accident I had an idea for a short film about a quadriplegic who lives in a dream. Long, long before I came to know and love Africa as a place, I yearned for it as an idea. In the fall of 1995, after resigning from my last academic

LISTS

IN THIS PASSAGE FROM HER JOURNAL ON GARDENING, HELEN DILLON WRITES ABOUT HER FAMILY'S PENCHANT FOR MAKING LISTS.

My mother makes lists. She got it from my grandmother, who made endless lists in a little red book that lived in the hall. I always knew when my grandmother was heading for the book, as the large bunch of keys attached to her person would jangle her approach through a series of banging doors. Surrounded by an aura of crossness and Mansion floor polish (which was constantly applied to the slidey oak floor) she would start muttering away and writing in the book.

My mother almost certainly makes lists of her lists. When feeling rattled about too many things to do, I've been known to write down things that've just been done, only to cross them off straight away – very therapeutic for the obsessive list maker (it gives the illusion of work in progress).

– Helen Dillon, *Helen Dillon On Gardening*

CAN YOU LIST . . .

YOUR FAVOURITE BOOKS?

FILMS YOU LOVED?

COUNTRIES YOU'VE VISITED?

PLACES YOU'D LIKE TO VISIT?

YOUR PROUDEST MOMENTS?

TEN PEOPLE WHO INSPIRE YOU?

PLAYS OR MUSICALS YOU ENJOYED?

SINGERS YOU ADMIRE?

MOMENTS YOU TREASURE?

ANY FUTURE PLANS?

YOUR FAVOURITE TV OR RADIO
PROGRAMMES?

YOUR FAVOURITE DAYS OF THE YEAR?

FILMS

1. ....

2. ....

3. ....

4. ....

5. ....

6. ....

7. ....

8. ....

9. ....

10. ....

1. ....

2. ....

3. ....

4. ....

5. ....

6. ....

7. ....

8. ....

9. ....

10. ....

10.

CITIES BANDS FILMS
CONCERTS SONGS
FRIENDS LOVES
BOSSES COMICS DAYS
MOMENTS PLACES
TIMES RESTAURANTS
MEALS PUBS TRIPS
PICNICS SINGERS
PARADES BIRTHDAYS
WINES EVENTS CARS
STREETS BISCUITS
PARKS BOOKS PLAYS

MUSIC

1. ....

2. ....

3. ....

4. ....

5. ....

6. ....

7. ....

8. ....

9. ....

10. ....

1. ....

2. ....

3. ....

4. ....

5. ....

6. ....

7. ....

8. ....

9. ....

10. ....

SONGS

1. ....

2. ....

3. ....

4. ....

5. ....

6. ....

7. ....

8. ....

9. ....

10. ....

	FRIENDS	HEROES
1.	1.	1. ....
2.	2.	2. ....
3.	3.	3. ....
4.	4.	4. ....
5.	5.	5. ....
6.	6.	6. ....
7.	7.	7. ....
8.	8.	8. ....
9.	9.	9. ....
10.	10.	10. ....

EVENTS

1. ....

2. ....

3. ....

4. ....

5. ....

6. ....

7. ....

8. ....

9. ....

10. ....

10.

CITIES BANDS FILMS
CONCERTS SONGS
FRIENDS LOVES
BOSSES COMICS DAYS
MOMENTS PLACES
TIMES RESTAURANTS
MEALS PUBS TRIPS
PICNICS SINGERS
PARADES BIRTHDAYS
WINES EVENTS CARS
STREETS BISCUITS
PARKS BOOKS PLAYS

1. ....

2. ....

3. ....

4. ....

5. ....

6. ....

7. ....

8. ....

9. ....

10. ....

10.

CITIES BANDS FILMS
CONCERTS SONGS
FRIENDS LOVES
BOSSES COMICS DAYS
MOMENTS PLACES
TIMES RESTAURANTS
MEALS PUBS TRIPS
PICNICS SINGERS
PARADES BIRTHDAYS
WINES EVENTS CARS
STREETS BISCUITS
PARKS BOOKS PLAYS

1. ....

2. ....

3. ....

4. ....

5. ....

6. ....

7. ....

8. ....

9. ....

10. ....

BOOKS

1. ....

2. ....

3. ....

4. ....

5. ....

6. ....

7. ....

8. ....

9. ....

10. ....

MOMENTS

1. ....
2. ....
3. ....
4. ....
5. ....
6. ....
7. ....
8. ....
9. ....
10. ....

1. ....
2. ....
3. ....
4. ....
5. ....
6. ....
7. ....
8. ....
9. ....
10. ....

PLACES

1. ....
2. ....
3. ....
4. ....
5. ....
6. ....
7. ....
8. ....
9. ....
10. ....

10.

CITIES BANDS FILMS
CONCERTS SONGS
FRIENDS LOVES
BOSSES COMICS DAYS
MOMENTS PLACES
TIMES RESTAURANTS
MEALS PUBS TRIPS
PICNICS SINGERS
PARADES BIRTHDAYS
WINES EVENTS CARS
STREETS BISCUITS
PARKS BOOKS PLAYS

DAYS

1. ....
2. ....
3. ....
4. ....
5. ....
6. ....
7. ....
8. ....
9. ....
10. ....

NAMES

1. ....
2. ....
3. ....
4. ....
5. ....
6. ....
7. ....
8. ....
9. ....
10. ....

ARTISTS

1. ....

2. ....

3. ....

4. ....

5. ....

6. ....

7. ....

8. ....

9. ....

10. ....

1. ....

2. ....

3. ....

4. ....

5. ....

6. ....

7. ....

8. ....

9. ....

10. ....

1. ....

2. ....

3. ....

4. ....

5. ....

6. ....

7. ....

8. ....

9. ....

10. ....

LOVES

1.	....
2.	....
3.	....
4.	....
5.	....
6.	....
7.	....
8.	....
9.	....
10.	....

1.	....
2.	....
3.	....
4.	....
5.	....
6.	....
7.	....
8.	....
9.	....
10.	....

1.	....
2.	....
3.	....
4.	....
5.	....
6.	....
7.	....
8.	....
9.	....
10.	....

CITIES

1. ....
2. ....
3. ....
4. ....
5. ....
6. ....
7. ....
8. ....
9. ....
10. ....

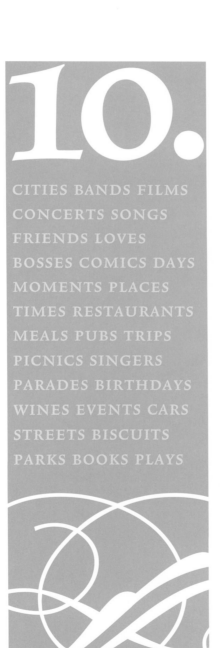

10.

CITIES BANDS FILMS
CONCERTS SONGS
FRIENDS LOVES
BOSSES COMICS DAYS
MOMENTS PLACES
TIMES RESTAURANTS
MEALS PUBS TRIPS
PICNICS SINGERS
PARADES BIRTHDAYS
WINES EVENTS CARS
STREETS BISCUITS
PARKS BOOKS PLAYS

1. ....
2. ....
3. ....
4. ....
5. ....
6. ....
7. ....
8. ....
9. ....
10. ....

TRACING YOUR FAMILY HISTORY
BY CAROLINE MULLAN

START YOUR SEARCH WITH

WHAT YOU KNOW.

YOU WILL BE AMAZED AT

WHAT YOU CAN DISCOVER

ONCE YOU GET GOING.

TALK TO RELATIVES.

Begin with the elderly but also talk to younger members of your extended family – everyone has something to contribute. Ask simple questions. Most people initially say they know nothing (*'If only your Uncle Ned were alive . . .'*) but every single person knows something of their family. Don't just rely on the stories you hear from one member of the family. Siblings differ, often vehemently, about the past but their collective memories can be very useful. A sure way to antagonise someone is to cast doubt or contradict their story. (*'But Aunt May says . . .'*). Keep listening – and get everyone's version.

A tape recorder is a good idea for various reasons. There is less pressure to write frantically or to ask those being interviewed to repeat their words. It makes transcribing into print much easier. It's also good to know that Granny's actual voice with her own accent and way of speaking is being

recorded for posterity. Show your written version of the recording for approval. This may even prove to be another opportunity for further jogged memories.

Besides family members, there are others who can be informative. Sometimes old neighbours of Great-Aunt Nelly may know of *'cousins called Jim and Nora McInerney from Ennis'* or recall that Granny reminisced regularly of her schooldays *'in the same school as my mother in Knocklofty.'*

Always enquire if there was a relation who called by or was spoken of although the exact relationship is now unknown: *'Uncle Tim from the North Circular Road . . . our cousin Hilda – I think her surname was Bennett . . . Daddy's cousins, the McAnaspies.'* Remember that, misleadingly, Mammy's best friend, Mary O'Hara, was often given the courtesy title of 'Aunt Mary', less formal than Mrs. O'Hara because children generally would not be allowed to address adults by their first names.

USEFUL ITEMS IN YOUR HOME

MEMORIAL CARDS
Granny's missal was full of them. Memorial cards can be very useful, but remember that the ages quoted aren't necessarily accurate.

FAMILY BIBLE
You may not still own the family Bible, but the births of your grandfather and his siblings may have been written in the Bible that is now in the possession of distant, maybe unknown as yet, cousins. Sometimes families also recorded immunisation details in the family Bible.

CERTIFICATES
If you can find birth, baptismal, marriage or death certificates, the information will be invaluable and usually accurate. Exam results, expired passports, professional qualifications and deeds showing ownership of graves are also helpful.

LETTERS

Letters are a rich source of family history with their news of events both personal and political. Because letters were often intended to be passed around to the extended family and neighbours, they may omit any darker aspects of the family history. Don't forget about old postcards, too.

GREETING CARDS

Birthday and anniversary cards can give clues to characters who played a part in your family's life ('Love, Auntie Nuala' or 'From all your cousins at Rathmore').

INSCRIPTIONS IN BOOKS

A simple inscription found in a book can sometimes clear up details: 'To Molly on her 10th birthday 15 June 1897' or 'Awarded to Mary McGowan for First Prize in English Composition, 4th Class 1919 Mercy Convent, Reenduagh'.

NEWSCUTTINGS, SCRAPBOOKS

Birth, marriage and death announcements; obituaries; court cases; local news – even if the names mentioned don't seem familiar they may refer to distant relatives, as yet unknown, or neighbours of the family long ago in another place. Newscuttings are usually kept for a good reason.

PHOTOGRAPHS

Sadly they rarely have names on the back, though clues to formal ones can be the photographer and city. They can often be dated by the clothes worn or by clues in the background of the photo, like the year or the make of an automobile.

GENERAL MEMORABILIA

Besides giving dates and addresses, old bills, receipts, theatre and sports programmes can add colour to the family story indicating what people ate (grocer's bill) and wore (milliner, draper, tailor) or pointing to pastimes – acting in plays or sports activities.

USEFUL AIDS IN FAMILY TRACING

There are various books and publications on tracing your family available in bookshops and libraries and also in outlets which sell family crests and family tree charts. There are advisors to help you in the Genealogical Service of the National Library and the National Archives.

NATIONAL LIBRARY

The National Library (Kildare Street, Dublin 2) holds Catholic baptismal and marriage records (very few parishes kept death records); *Griffith's Valuation*; tithe applotments, directories, printed family histories and old photograph collections.

NATIONAL ARCHIVES

In the National Archives (Bishop Street, Dublin 2) you will find census records, indexes to wills, *Griffith's Valuation* (see p. 263) and records of government departments. The *Chief Secretary's Office Report to Parliament* (CSORP) papers, often referred to as the 'Outrage Papers', may not sound relevant but can often yield valuable information. These are essentially police reports of both serious and minor crimes. However, many people in 19th century Ireland were involved in political matters such as protests against evictions or in Land War activities and it is possible to find family names and details. These are indexed under surname, place or subject.

CENSUS RECORDS

The Irish census records of 1901 and 1911 are the only ones available for research (earlier census records were destroyed although some fragments exist: later ones are not yet released) and are available for viewing on microfilm in the National Archives. The ages given, except for children, are not necessarily accurate – Granny might have admitted to being 29 in 1901 but to 36 in 1911.

CIVIL RECORDS

Civil records of births, marriages and deaths are available in Joyce House, Lombard Street, Dublin 2. Civil registration began in Ireland in 1864 but non-Catholic marriages were registered from 1845. Photocopies of the original records are available for research purposes and are much less expensive than actual certificates, which are legal documents.

PARISH RECORDS

Roman Catholic, Church of Ireland, Presbyterian, Methodist and Quaker records are kept in different records offices (National Library; Representative Church Body of Ireland; Public Record Office of Northern Ireland; Library of the Society of Friends, Dublin) and are usually held locally. Baptismal records very often give the date of birth. Deaths were not often noted in parish records. For Jewish records contact The Irish Jewish Museum, 3 Walworth Road, Dublin 8.

WILLS

The fire in the Four Courts during the Civil War in 1923 destroyed many records. The indexes give useful information and are available in the National Archives. Some families have a solicitor who has dealt with their affairs for many years and who may hold wills. It's worth asking relatives whether such a person or firm is known.

GRIFFITH'S VALUATION 1851

This document contains the names of occupants of land, and includes important information relating to location, acreage and landlords. Microfilms can be viewed at the National Archives, the National Library, and other records offices. The only names given are those of the main occupant and his/her immediate landlord.

THE VALUATION OFFICE

The Valuation Office, located in the Irish Life Building, Dublin 1, holds the notebooks of *Griffith's Valuation* surveyors with detailed notes on fields, buildings, etc. It is also possible to follow occupancy through changes over the years right up to the present.

TITHE APPLOTMENTS 1823-1838

Here you can find lists of the main occupants of lands and the names of landlords. They were originally used to levy tithes for the Established Church. Microfilms can be viewed at the National Archives, National Library and other records offices.

LAND RECORDS

The Registry of Deeds, Henrietta Street, Dublin 1, stores leases, mortgages and marriage settlements. These are of limited use but are always worth checking. The records are indexed by surname and also by place name.

CEMETERIES

Gravestones or cemetery records are useful. The date of death is usually needed to make enquiry to the cemetery office if there is no gravestone. There are also listings of grave inscriptions for some areas (Brian J. Cantwell's *Memorials of the Dead* covers Wexford and Wicklow) available in the National Library, the National Archives and in some local libraries. Many cemetery records are also available on the Internet.

LIBRARIES

You can visit the National Library of Ireland, City and County Libraries, reference libraries and the local history/genealogy section in local libraries. Librarians are usually knowledgeable and helpful.

MILITARY RECORDS

Army, navy and airforce records are useful for birth date, birthplace, parents' names and education.

SCHOOL/COLLEGE RECORDS

Brief details are sometimes available from school annuals or published histories of schools or colleges.

WORKPLACE RECORDS

Some companies, such as Guinness, have very comprehensive records of employees. Records also exist for teachers (Department of Education), the police (Royal Irish Constabulary, Dublin Metropolitan Police) and railway employees (Irish Transport Genealogical Archives, Irish Railway Record Society, Heuston Station, Dublin 8).

PROFESSIONAL ASSOCIATIONS

If your relatives worked in any of the professions, you can look into the appropriate professional association. For example, information on doctors' qualifications are held in the Royal College of Surgeons in Ireland and in the Royal College of Physicians in Ireland. Lawyers' records can be found in *Kings Inns Admission Papers 1723-1867*, available at the National Library.

NEWSPAPERS

Newspapers can be consulted for birth, marriage, death announcements and obituaries. They can also be a source of relevant information on events that the family may have been involved in, not necessarily mentioned by name (evictions, political rallies, shipwrecks, court cases). There is a good selection of local newspapers available in the National Library and a large collection (including Irish papers) in the British Library Newspaper Library, Colindale Avenue, London NW9 5HE.

DIRECTORIES

Thom's Dublin Directory, General Post Office directories, *Slater's* and *Pigot's* are all available in the National Library (some are available in the National Archives and on the Internet). *Manuscript Sources for the Study of Irish Civilisation* (ed. Richard Hayes) indexes all kinds of documents chronologically with reference numbers under persons, places and dates. This is a useful source for family history.

LOCAL GENEALOGY/FAMILY HISTORY SOCIETIES

Useful tips, help and encouragement can be gained by talking to other members of local history and genealogical societies or by attending their lectures.

THE INTERNET

The Internet is a very useful resource, but only if you know enough to recognise what you are looking for. If children are using the Internet, they should be supervised by an adult.

BOOKS

Tracing Your Irish Ancestors, the Complete Guide by John Grenham, Gill & Macmillan, 2006
Tracing Irish Ancestors, a Practical Guide to Irish Genealogy by Máire MacConghail and Paul Gorry, Collins, 1997
Irish Records: Sources for Family & Local History by James G. Ryan, Salt Lake City, 1997

FOR THOSE OUTSIDE IRELAND

Consult church and civil records, censuses, wills, land records, cemeteries, military records, schools, colleges, workplaces, and newspapers in England, USA, Canada, Australia, New Zealand, before starting on Irish records. All of these places have good records. You can go online to find out where to locate them or check the many publications on family research published in these countries.

SHIPPING, NATURALISATION, AND IMMIGRATION RECORDS

All of these records are becoming more easily available and are being indexed by government agencies, family history societies etc. The simplest method is to check online. For example, there is an Ellis Island website.

Happy searching!

YOUR FAMILY TREE

THERE ARE MANY WAYS TO MAKE A FAMILY TREE. HERE ARE TWO EXAMPLES OF HOW IT CAN BE DONE. USE THIS PAGE AS A MASTER. PUT YOURSELF AT THE TOP AND THEN FILL IN AS MANY OF THE BLANKS AS YOU CAN. LABEL THIS PAGE NUMBER ONE. THEN, MAKE ANOTHER CHART WITH YOUR MOTHER AT THE TOP (AND LABEL IT PAGE NUMBER TWO) AND A THIRD CHART WITH YOUR GRANDMOTHER AT THE TOP, AND SO ON. BY CONSULTING FAMILY MEMBERS YOU SHOULD BE ABLE TO BUILD A COMPREHENSIVE FAMILY TREE.

IF YOU'RE FEELING CREATIVE YOU COULD USE THE PAGE AT THE RIGHT AND DO SOMETHING SIMILAR. IT MIGHT BE FUN TO PUT PORTRAITS OF YOUR FAMILY ON THE TREE.

MY NAME:

BORN ON:

WHERE:

MARRIED TO:

WHEN:

DIED ON:

WHERE:

SIBLINGS

_____

_____

_____

_____

_____

MOTHER

NAME:

BORN ON:

WHERE:

MARRIED TO:

WHEN:

DIED ON:

WHERE:

FATHER

NAME:

BORN ON:

WHERE:

MARRIED TO:

WHEN:

DIED ON:

WHERE:

GRANDMOTHER

NAME:

BORN ON:

WHERE:

MARRIED TO:

WHEN:

DIED ON:

WHERE:

GRANDFATHER

NAME:

BORN ON:

WHERE:

MARRIED TO:

WHEN:

DIED ON:

WHERE:

GRANDMOTHER

NAME:

BORN ON:

WHERE:

MARRIED TO:

WHEN:

DIED ON:

WHERE:

GRANDFATHER

NAME:

BORN ON:

WHERE:

MARRIED TO:

WHEN:

DIED ON:

WHERE:

CREDITS

FAMILY STORY
p. 26: Extract from *An Only Child* and *My Father's Son* by Frank O'Connor, Penguin Books, 2005
Copyright © Frank O'Connor, 2005
p. 28: First line of *An Evil Cradling* by Brian Keenan, Vintage, London, 1993
p. 30: First line of *The Story of My Life* by Helen Keller, Dover Publications, New York 1996
p. 32: First line of *Donkey's Years* by Aidan Higgins, Martin Secker & Warburg Ltd, London, 1999
p. 34: First line of *All of These People* by Fergal Keane, Harper Perennial, London, 2006
p. 36: First line of *Never Have Your Dog Stuffed* by Alan Alda, Hutchinson, London, 2006

PORTRAITS
p. 40: Extract from *In the Dark Room* by Brian Dillon, Penguin Books, 2005. Copyright © Brian Dillon, 2005
p. 42: First line of *Angela's Ashes* by Frank McCourt, Harper Perennial, London, 2004
p. 44: First line of *John Major, the Autobiography* by John Major, Harper Collins Publishers, London, 1999
p. 46: First line of *Wild Swans* by Jung Chang, Flamingo, London, 1993
p. 48: First line of *If I Don't Write It, Nobody Else Will* by Eric Sykes, Harper Perennial, London, 2006

EARLY YEARS
p. 52: Extract from *Memoir* by John McGahern, Faber and Faber Limited, London, 2005
p. 54: First line of *Sand In My Shoes – Memories of a Man from Rush* by Niall Weldon, Ashfield Press, Dublin, 2005
p. 56: First line of *My Life* by Bill Clinton, Hutchinson, London, 2004
p. 58: First line of *My Life So Far* by Jane Fonda, Ebury Press, London, 2006

GROWING UP
p. 62: Extract from *Vive Moi!* by Sean O'Faolain, Sinclair-Stevenson, London, 1993. Copyright © 1963 Sean O'Faolain. Reproduced by permission of the estate of Sean O'Faolain c/o Rogers, Coleridge & White Ltd., 20 Powis Mews, London W11 1JN.
p. 64: First line of *The Speckled People* by Hugo Hamilton, Harper Perennial, London, 2004
p. 66: First line of *Pelé, the Autobiography* by Pelé with Orlando Duarte and Alex Bellos, Simon & Schuster UK, London, 2006
p. 68: First line of *Oughtobiography* by David Marcus, Gill & Macmillan Ltd, Dublin, 2001

LEAVING
p. 72: Extract from *An Evil Cradling* by Brian Keenan, published by Hutchinson. Reprinted by permission of The Random House Group Ltd.
p. 74: First line of *In the Firing Line* by Brian Mawhinney, HarperCollins Publishers, London, 1999
p. 76: First line of *My Father's Son* by Frank O'Connor, Penguin Books, London, 2005
p. 78: First line of *Point of Departure* by James Cameron, Granta Books, London, 2006

FRIENDS
p. 82: Extract from *The Rocky Years* by Ferdia Mac Anna, Hodder Headline Ireland, Dublin, 2004
p. 84: First line of *And Why Not?* by Barry Norman, Pocket Books, London, 2003
p. 86: First line of *Time Added On, The Autobiography* by George Hook, Penguin Ireland, Dublin, 2005
p. 88: First line of *On the Road* by Shay Healy, The O'Brien Press Limited, Dublin, 2005
p. 90: First line of *Hurler On the Ditch* by Michael Mills, Currach Press, Dublin, 2005

LOVES
p. 94: Extract from *Follow Your Dream* by Daniel O'Donnell, published by The O'Brien Press Ltd., Dublin, © Copyright Daniel O'Donnell
p. 96: First line of *Is That It?* by Bob Geldof with Paul Vallely, Pan Macmillan Ltd, London, 2005

p. 98: First line of *A Warring Absence* by Caitlin Thomas with George Tremlett, Pan Books, 1987

p. 100: First line of *A Mother's Story* by Sara Payne with Anna Gekoski, Hodder & Stoughton, London, 2004

p. 102: First line of the prologue to *Loving George* by Alex Best, John Blake Publishing Ltd, London, 2006

ANIMALS

p. 106: Extract from *To School Through the Fields* by Alice Taylor, Brandon, Dingle, Co. Kerry, 1998

p. 108: First line of *Marley & Me* by John Grogan, Hodder & Stoughton, London, 2006

p. 110: First line of *Desert Flower* by Waris Dirie with Cathleen Miller, Virago Press, 2006

PLACES

p. 114: Extract from *Angela's Ashes* by Frank McCourt. Reprinted by permission of HarperCollins Publishers Ltd. © Frank McCourt, 2004

p. 116: *Deoraíocht le Pádraic Ó Conaire; An Comhlacht Oideachais, Baile Átha Cliath, 1994*

p. 118: First line of *Memoir* by John McGahern, Faber and Faber Limited, London, 2005

p. 120: First line of *Bonfires on the Hillside* by James Kelly, Fountain Publishing, Belfast, 1995

TRAVEL

p. 124: Extract from *Paul Durcan's Diary* by Paul Durcan, New Island, Dublin, 2003

p. 126: First line of *Homage to Barcelona* by Colm Tóibín, Picador, London, 2002

p. 128: First line of *Full Tilt* by Dervla Murphy, John Murray (Publishers), London, 2004

p. 130: First line of *Stranger on a Train* by Jenny Diski, Virago Press, London, 2004

p. 132: First line of *A Year in the Centre* by Brian O'Driscoll, Penguin Ireland, Dublin, 2005

EDUCATION

p. 136: Extract from *The Time of My Life* by Gay Byrne, with Deirdre Purcell, is reproduced with the permission of the publishers, Gill & Macmillan, Dublin

p. 138: First line of *In My Father's House* by Seán Dunne, The Gallery Press, Oldcastle, Co. Meath, 2000

p. 140: First line of *Twenty Years A-Growing* by Maurice O'Sullivan, Oxford Paperbacks, Oxford, 1983

p. 142: First line of *Where There's A Will* by John Mortimer, Penguin Books, London, 2004

p. 144: First line of *That Day's Struggle, A Memoir 1904-1951* by Sean MacBride, edited by Catriona Lawlor, Currach Press, Dublin, 2005

WORK

p. 148: Extract from *Nell* by Nell McCafferty, Penguin Books Ireland, 2004. Copyright © Nell McCafferty, 2004

p 150: First line of *Words* by Jean-Paul Sartre, Penguin Books, London, 2000

p 152: First line of *Living History* by Hillary Rodham Clinton, Headline Book Publishing, London, 2004

p 154: First line of *Paper Tigers* by Mary Kennedy, Merlin Publishing, Dublin, 2003

p 156: First line of *Passing Through* by Declan Hassett, Mercier Press, 2004

CELEBRATIONS

p. 160: Extract from *Misadventures in Motherhood* by Fiona Looney, published by The O'Brien Press Ltd., Dublin, © Copyright Fiona Looney

p. 162: First line of *Rogue Trader* by Nick Leeson with Edward Whitley, Time Warner Books, London, 2006

p. 164: First line of *Not Quite the Diplomat* by Chris Patten, Allen Lane, London, 2005

FAITH

p. 168: Extract from *The Sign of the Cross* by Colm Tóibín, Vintage, London, 1995. Copyright © Colm Toibin. Reproduced by permission of the author c/o Rogers, Coleridge & White Ltd., 20 Powis Mews, London W11 1JN.

p. 170: First line of *Another Country* by Gene Kerrigan, Gill and Macmillan Ltd, Dublin 1998

p. 172: First line of *Confessio* by St Patrick as published in *Patrick in His Own Words* by Joseph Duffy, Veritas, Dublin, 1985

p. 174: First line of *My Stamp on Life* by Max Stern, Makor Jewish Community Library, Victoria, Australia, 2003

SPORT

p. 178: Extract from *Dún Síon to Croke Park* by Micheál Ó Muircheartaigh, Penguin Books, 2004, 2005. Copyright © Micheál Ó Muircheartaigh, 2004

p. 180: First line of *Fever Pitch* by Nick Hornby, Victor Gollancz, London, 1993

p. 182: First line of *Hard Tackles and Dirty Baths* by George Best with Harry Harris, Ebury Press, London, 2006

p184: First line of *Touching the Void* by Joe Simpson, Vintage, London, 1997

p. 186: First line of *Over the Bar* by Breandán Ó hEithir, The Collins Press, Cork, 2005

PASTIMES

p. 190: Extract from *My Left Foot* by Christy Brown. Published by Chatto & Windus. Reprinted by permission of The Random House Group Ltd.

p. 192: First line of *Chronicles – Volume One* by Bob Dylan, Pocket Books, London, 2005

p. 194: First line of *Helen Dillon On Gardening* by Helen Dillon, TownHouse, Dublin, 2005

p. 196: First line of *A Year In Provence* by Peter Mayle, Penguin Books, London, 2000

p. 198: First line of *Rory & Ita* by Roddy Doyle, Vintage Books, London, 2002

CITIZENSHIP

p. 202: Extract from *The Speckled People* by Hugo Hamilton. Reprinted by permission of HarperCollins Publishers Ltd. © Hugo Hamilton, 2004.

p. 204: First line of *Freedom In Exile* by The Dalai Lama, Abacus, London, 2005

p. 206: First line of *Memoirs* by Jean Monnet, Doubleday & Company, Inc., New York, 1978

p. 208: First line of *Willie John – The Story of My Life* by Willie John McBride and Peter Bills, Portrait, London, 2005

p. 210: First line of *Summer Meditations* by Václav Havel, Faber and Faber, London, 1992

TURNING POINTS

p. 214: Extract from *Is That It?* by Bob Geldof with Paul Vallely, Pan Macmillan, London, 2005

p. 216: First line of *A Very Easy Death* by Simone de Beauvoir, Penguin Books, London,1969

p. 218: First line of *My Lives* by Edmund White, Bloomsbury Publishing plc, London, 2005

p. 220: First line of *Next to You* by Gloria Hunniford, Michael Joseph, London, 2005

DREAMS

p. 224: Extract from *Bridge Across My Sorrows* by Christina Noble with Robert Coram, Corgi Books, London, 1995. Reproduced by permission of John Murray (Publishers) Ltd.

p. 226: First line of *Still Me* by Christopher Reeve, Arrow Books, London, 1999

p. 228: First line of *A Passage to Africa* by George Alagiah, Time Warner Paperbacks, London, 2002

p. 230: First line of *Reading Lolita in Tehran, A Memoir in Books* by Azar Nafisi, Fourth Estate, London, 2004

SECRETS

p. 234: Extract from *Almost There: The Onward Journey of a Dublin Woman* by Nuala O'Faolain, Michael Joseph, 2003, Penguin Books, 2004. Copyright © Nuala O'Faolain, 2003

p. 236: First line of *A Brother's Journey*, by Richard B. Pelzer, Time Warner Books, London, 2005

p. 238: *Mo Bhealach Féin le Seosamh MacGrianna*, An Gúm, Foras na Gaeilge, Baile Atha Cliath, 2004

p. 240: First line of *The Diary of a Young Girl* by Anne Frank, Penguin Books, London, 1997

p. 242: First line of *My Ear At His Heart* by Hanif Kureishi, Faber and Faber Limited, London, 2004

LISTS

p. 246: Extract from *Helen Dillon On Gardening* by Helen Dillon, TownHouse, Dublin, 2005

ACKNOWLEDGMENTS

EDITOR
John Waters

DESIGNER
Ed Miliano

EDITORIAL COORDINATOR
Caroline Lynch

PROOFREADER
Emer Connolly

PROJECT TEAM
Maryrose Barrington (Chair), Anne-Marie Butler, Caroline Lynch, Ed Miliano, Críona Murray
Eugene Murray, Emer O'Riordan, Eileen Pearson and John Waters

THANKS TO
Babcock and Browne, Marion Gunn, Eleanor McCarthy, Mary Millea, Caroline Mullan, Bill Shipsey
and Gordon Snell

SPECIAL THANKS TO
Maeve Binchy